KICK IN THE PANTS

Therapy

The Anthology of the PsychoIllogical Bulletin Volumes 1- 6

Edited by David J. Robinson, M.D.
Illustrated by Brian Chapman

Rapid Psychler Press

Rapid Psychler Press

P.O. Box 596305
Fort Gratiot, Michigan
USA 48059-6305

P.O. Box 8117
London, Ontario
Canada N6G 2B0

Toll Free Phone 888-PSY-CHLE (888-779-2453)
Toll Free Fax 888-PSY-CHLR (888-779-2457)
Outside U.S. & Canada — Fax 519-657-9753
website: www.psychler.com
email: psychler@psychler.com

ISBN 0-9680324-4-3
Printed in The United States of America
© 1997, Rapid Psychler Press
First Edition, First Printing

Dedication

This book is dedicated to my closest friends:

Dean Avola, Brad Groshok, Tom Kay & Mark Kennedy

for their advice, encouragement and for keeping in touch across the time and distance that separates us.

I would also like to give a special acknowledgment to **Brian Chapman** for his excellent illustrations and to all the authors for contributing their work.

Editor's Foreword

My last purely creative accomplishment was in 1969. I won an award in grade school for a painting of an astronaut preparing to land on a planet. Although the lunar landing was the hot news item, I clearly recall this poor voyager attempting a solar landing, because yellow suited the picture better. In the ensuing years, I got caught up in scholarship, with science and academic standing becoming the focus of my efforts.

I didn't find that medical school particularly prized individuality or creativity in its students. I have fond memories of a classmate who waged a quiet rebellion on the "system." Though he was truly a class act, the school won more battles than it lost.

I chose psychiatry for many reasons, one of the most important being that it seemed to be the most humane of all the medical specialties. It continues to puzzle me that this expectation both has and has not borne itself out. Psychiatrists are a paradox. Some have remarkable abilities with not only with their depth of understanding, but in their abilities to help others. Others are so uncomfortable in dealing with people they squirm until they can write a prescription. What particularly baffles me is the way that psychiatry deals with humor. Comedy is reliably Hollywood's most bankable product. There are many studies, books and proponents of the physical and psychological benefits of laughter. While books on medical humor abound, few deal specifically with psychiatric humor. I am at a loss to understand how psychiatrists can be balanced enough to help others unless they have a sense of humor and use it in their work. For this reason, I started the *Psycholllogical Bulletin* (PIB) in 1994.

Support and criticism have come unpredictably. One senior forensic psychiatrist from Alberta, Canada was so indignant that he "reported" me to a licensing body because I sent him a free copy of Volume 1. From now on, he'll have to pay. The PIB got a major boost once it crossed the border. It now has hundreds of subscribers and is popular enough to warrant publishing this anthology. It has been very rewarding to see the efforts of those involved amount to a collection of satirical articles which is impressive in both its range of topics and variety of humor styles.

Enjoy, and Keep Psychling!

Dave Robinson   May, 1997
                         London, Ontario, Canada

The Rapid Psychlers

- **Brian & Fanny Chapman**, both fine and food artists

- **Dean Avola**, marketing whiz with strong ideas and a strong back

- **Dr. Donna Robinson**, promotion and sisterly duties, and **Dr. Rob Bauer** (multi-faceted help from a cardiologist's perspective)

- **Monty & Lil Robinson**, for helping with all aspects of this venture, for being great parents, and for conceiving me in the first place

- **Mark & Nicole Kennedy**, for taking care of all the big things, all the little things, and always helping out when I'm in over my head (blub . . . blub . . .)

- **Brad Groshok** (Odyssey Network Inc. & Quality Computer Systems), for being there at midnight when the computer crashes, and for making my productivity a priority

- **Kathi Sword & Glenn Avola**, marketing & graphics support

- **Tom Norry**, **Janice Seaborn**, **Sue Fletcher** & **Dr. Sandra Northcott**, proof and spoof readers

- **Mary-Ann McLean** and **Alex McFadden**, my special "kitchen sink" crew

- **Jan Macdonald**, for design of the Rapid Psychler website

- **Gabrielle Bauer**, for editing the manuscript and making numerous helpful suggestions (email: drewgabi@interlog.com)

- **Dr. Glenn Ellenbogen**, from the *Journal of Polymorphous Perversity*, for the advice and support along the way

- **Dr. Quentin Rae-Grant**, for his encouragement and for giving me the exposure and contacts so I didn't have to keep writing all the articles myself

- **Dr. Harold Merskey** and **Dr. John Mount**, for being excellent clinicians and for keeping a sense of humor about your work

I would also like to acknowledge the following for keeping me company:
- *Kenny G*, *Richard Elliot*, *Dave Koz*, *Warren Hill*, and *Nelson Rangell*, for the great sax playing which kept me inspired.
- *Coca-Cola*, for the great-tasting, caffeinated beverage that kept me awake.

Table of Contents

Section X: Holidays, Gifts & Miscellaneous Ads*   165

Other Rapid Psychler Products¶

* Ads for products in this section are strictly satire, these items don't exist.

¶ Rapid Psychler Press produces both educational and humorous publications. We have an expanding line of textbooks that include an "edutainment" presentation, but are otherwise "serious" texts. Products in this section are available from Rapid Psychler Press and many bookstores.
See page 2 for information on how to contact us.

Section I
Psychotherapy

"This is just a temporary bandaid cure. You'll need
years of therapy later in life to completely recover."

Towards a Therapeutic Synthesis:
Kick-in-the-Pants Therapy

David J. Robinson, M.D.

Introduction
The unparalleled popularity of *Fly-by-the-Seat-of-Your-Pants* **Therapy** [1] and its major clinical derivative **Ventilation Therapy** [2] provided the impetus for further research into new therapeutic interventions. Based on these models, the features of other current therapies were synthesized into a new modality, called *Kick-in-the-Pants* **Therapy** (KITPT). Early reports show promising results in the areas of clinical efficacy, client efficiency and cost effectiveness (the three 'C-E' factors invented by some TQM wizard).

Technique
The application of KITPT consists of three stages:

1. As per the above time-tested techniques, the therapist becomes either an aviator or ventilator and collects information to the point where the patient takes responsibility for some part of his or her dilemma. In the case of extreme resistance, launch a pre-emptive interpretation and insist that the patient's behavior is guilt-based. Then, use their immediate reply as evidence.

2. Drawing on the tenets of **Gestalt** & **Advice Therapies**, the therapist then includes a fundamental existential truth, such as:

• There are several good decaffeinated brands out there, try one!
• If you can't stand the heat, get out of the oven!
• Until you're the lead dog, the view never changes!

3. Applying the practical benefits of **Behavioral** & **Reality-Based Therapies**, the patient assumes a flexed posture and is administered a swift kick in the pants. Extensive experience on the receiving side of this therapeutic exchange leads the author to suggest that a force of between 90—200 foot-pounds be applied to the lateral gluteal area. Therapists with prior punting or place-kicking experience are advised to be deconditioned before trying this.

Comment
The results have been promising and show an unrivaled level of popular support.[3] KITPT produces the most rapid transference manifestations of any current therapy, and has been reliable in dislodging unconscious material. It effectively dissipates countertransference, thereby reducing the burden of practicing therapists taking up all the good time slots of supervising therapists.

KITPT Applications
• Prodding along constipated anal retentives
• Turning hindsight into insight
• Adding to any current therapy that has become impacted [4]

The number of single-session cures continues to grow. KITPT also provides a quantifiable measure of dedication to therapy, opening the door for statistical evaluations. Though this approach is still in its infancy, early results are encouraging. Unlike the therapy itself, there is no end in sight.

References

[1] Trial, A. & Error, B.
Journal of Impetuous Therapeutic Aviation and Navigation
Fly-By-Night Publishers; High Altitude, Colorado

[2] Chit & Chat
Verbiage Weekly
Free Association Promotions; Checkout Counter City, California

[3] Lay & Laity
Common Sense Quarterly
Restricted Circulation Press; Show-me, Missouri

[4] Ina Quagmire & Ima Stuck
Bulletin of Dead-End Therapies
Gegenhalten Press; No Haven, Connecticut

Fledgling Therapist Disorder

Daniel E. Shapiro, Ph.D.
Tucson, Arizona

The essential feature of **Fledgling Therapist Disorder** (FTD) is that it is initiated and maintained in response to the anxiety of being a novice therapist. In the early stages of the disorder, the individual typically is unable to distinguish how therapy is different from ordinary social interactions. Understanding that they are supposed to do something, individuals with FTD may engage in numerous behaviors that they have heard or read about. These behaviors are varied and range from wearing a white lab coat and growing a beard to trying desperately to quickly fix any problem that the client presents. Individuals with FTD may become obsessed with the details of therapy. For example, many fledglings report being confused about how to look at their watches without seeming to be uninterested in the client. They also frequently become distressed when asked to discuss finances with their clients. Fortunately, with additional work and some direct yet gentle supervision, most symptoms of FTD resolve after about four or five years.

Age of onset. Varies, but the typical range is the mid to late twenties.

Course. Typically, therapists outgrow symptoms of FTD after approximately four to five years of conducting therapy and working under supervision. The disorder is frequently limited to one prolonged period, though persistent recurrences are relatively common. Some individuals never recover from FTD.

Predisposing factors. Individuals who are unable to imagine themselves ever needing or potentially benefiting from therapy usually develop more profound and chronic cases of FTD.

Prevalence. Every great therapist was once a beginner. Every great therapist once suffered from FTD. Some features of the disorder are found in all first-time therapists. Those who do not overtly show symptoms of FTD are probably suffering from *Supervisoraphobia*.

Originally published in the **Journal of Mental Health Counseling**
Vol. 17, Number 4, p. 456-461, October 1995. Reprinted with permission.

Diagnostic Criteria for Fledgling Therapist Disorder (FTD)

At some time during the disturbance, five or more of the following symptoms occur:

1. Saying "Wow, you're in bad shape! You should really see someone . ."

2. Overwhelming preoccupation with what to say or ask next.

3. Fierce desire to share personal information with the client.

4. Inability to tolerate silence during the session.

5. Desire to solve all of the client's difficulties in the first session.

6. Fear of being exposed for the fraud she or he is; excessive beliefs that she or he was accepted to graduate school in an accident involving the cosmos, the Postal Service, or the registrar's office.

7. Fear of looking at one's watch during sessions.

8. Fear of entering a cab only to find one's most disturbed client behind the wheel (sometimes the client's entire family is also in the cab).

9. Inability to function as a therapist without one or more of the following: white lab coat, clipboard, or pencil (previously categorized as **Untherapeutic Item Dependence — UID**).

10. Fear of charging for services rendered. Individuals with FTD often report the dreadful feeling of, "I wouldn't pay to see me in therapy!"

11. Desire to grow a beard to look more "therapeutic" (occurs regardless of gender). This characteristic is frequently accompanied by overuse of the chin-stroking technique.

12. Belief that if a client misses an appointment, the therapist must have failed during the previous session (therefore failing as a human being), and that shortly the earth will stop rotating on its axis.

13. Recognition that one is experiencing more anxiety than the client and that one would not mind changing places.

14. Hyper-Rogerianisms (the overuse of reflection)
Client: Do you have any coffee?
Therapist: I hear you saying that you want coffee.
Client: Yes, I would like some coffee.
Therapist: You are adamant about having coffee.
Client: Get me coffee or die.
Therapist: (while looking at watch) Oops, look at that decade, the late 90's already! Our time is up.

Fledgling Therapist With Supervisoraphobia Disorder (FTSD)

A. Meets criteria for Fledgling Therapist Disorder.

B. *Supervisoraphobia* is defined by fear of the following: being exposed as a fraud, being dismissed from graduate school, having one's undergraduate degree rescinded, and having one's supervisor contact one's mother to tell that her child turned out to be an overwhelming failure.

C. Presence of at least three of the following symptoms:

1. Immediate poor recall of critical details relevant to the therapy session, including the client's verbalizations, affect, and name.

2. Immediate poor recall of critical details relevant to the therapy session, including the therapist's verbalizations, affect, and name.

3. Diminished ability to operate a tape recorder properly, especially volume and record controls; and making statements such as "Darn, this was my best session ever but I taped your lecture right over it!"

4. Over-reliance on MBNT (Misleading Brown-Nosing Technique), including excessive head nodding, inappropriate use of the words "Yeah, now I get it," or "Golly, you know so much, it must be hard being you!"

5. Desperately engaging in discussions about any topic of interest to the supervisor, including hobbies, family life, and obscure research, just before playing the tapes of one's therapy session.

6. Obsessive preoccupation with everything one's supervisor says.

7. Having the uneasy feeling (after describing an interaction with a client to one's supervisor) that the description of the intervention sounded far more articulate than what actually took place.

D. Not superimposed on New M.A./M.S.W./Ph.D./M.D. disease.

Severity Specifiers for Fledgling Therapist With Supervisoraphobia

Mild: Few symptoms in excess of those required to make the diagnosis, and the symptoms result in mild impairment, for example, stuttering and stammering before describing the session.

Moderate: Functional impairment between mild and severe.

Severe: Symptoms in excess of those required to make the diagnosis, and marked interference both during therapy and during supervision as evidenced by statements to the client including "Would you mind if we switched places today?" In particularly distressing cases, fledgling therapists may try to write funny articles to compensate for their fears.

A Comparison of Therapeutic Technique

Carolyn Sullins, M.S.
Champaign, Illinois

With the increasing popularity of "borrowing" treatment interventions, the boundaries between various therapeutic schools are becoming less clear. In an attempt to illustrate the essence of the distinct styles, the author presents the response of various schools of thought to a client who says, "**I feel like shit**."

Client-Centered Therapist: *"So, you say you feel like shit right now."*

Psychoanalyst: *"You're anally fixated."*

Behavioral Therapist: *"We must desensitize you to shit. We'll pair it with a primary reinforcer, like food."*

Psychopharmacologist: *"Try 20mg of Prozac and 100cc of Pepto-Bismol daily."*

R.E.T.: *"You do NOT feel like shit! Shit feels wet and mushy."*

Existentialist: *"How can you find meaning and purpose in shit?"*

New Age Therapist: *"Get in touch with your shit. . . Now start to feel it in your body . . . Be the shit."*

Cognitive Therapist: *"We must learn more about this shit, let's record our thoughts and then we'll work it out with a pencil."*

Toward, Over, Under and Behind
A Theory for the Prediction of the Rehabilitation of Delinquent Behavior

James M. Stedman, Ph.D.
San Antonio, Texas

Since the Gluecks' pioneering work in the area of delinquency, researchers have been relentless in their quest for knowledge of the ways of wayward youth. Even Hunter Thompson's penetrating study of the Hell's Angels failed to produce additional insight into the mental setup of motorized teenage (and older) criminals. Predicting their rehabilitation has been even more difficult. As the daily news loudly proclaims, mutant teenage action-junkies proliferate and will bash you over the head, steal your wheels, or carry off your VCR simply for the exercise. Rehabilitation efforts cry out for a model which can differentiate the terminal teenage criminal from one willing to give up his or her twisted and unrestrained criminal behavior.

I believe that I have devised a foolproof, one-hundred percent predictive model for estimating which mutant teenage action-junkies can be rehabilitated, and which youths are likely to continue their "lifestyles of the twisted and infamous." This model was derived partially from intellectualization and partially from rationalization. My predictive theory is this: **"If a deviant youth, of his or her own volition, signs up to take Latin in the freshman year of high school, then that deviant can be rehabilitated by the normal means of probation officer supervision."**

To date, this model has been tested only on an n of 1; however, its predictive power has proven to be 100%. The subject in question was a gang member, a car thief, and an indulger in sex, drugs & rock 'n roll. Hence, he met all the criteria for Conduct Disorder Plus. When encountered, he was beginning his rehabilitation within the juvenile justice system. Shortly after beginning this process, Cicero Doe met the criteria for entry into the study by signing up to take Latin. Since Cicero was the first to enter the study, his course was followed with enthusiasm, albeit at a scientifically safe distance. I am happy to report his complete rehabilitation, including discontinued gang banging, restitution of the vehicle (with a full tank of gas) and his proclaimed academic motivation to become a professor of Symbolic Logic at Ft. Hay's State. QED — a totally successful prediction!

As with all research, in-depth interviewing of subjects is important and was not neglected in the current study. An excerpt from an interview with Cicero is recorded verbatim below.

Interviewer: Quousque' tandem Cicero, abutere patientia nostril?

Cicero: Nunc cogito quod civus republicae sum et quod in modo contra-alto naturam joe pesci contra civitatem.

Interviewer: Certe! Rectus! Et quo cum vitamin suam vadis?

Cicero: Morem depravatuum meam desistebo et philosophum, qui in rerun contemplatine studly ponit, flim-flam.

Translation

Interviewer: How long, Cicero, are you going to be a pain in the butt?

Cicero: Now, I know I'm a righteous dude (a.k.a. citizen) and that I've acted like a sleazeball.

Interviewer: Yeah! Right! And what are you going to do?

Cicero: I'll quit being a sleazeball and become a philosopher-dude

---

Cicero's responses demonstrate beyond a shadow of scientific doubt that his rehabilitation is complete. Obviously sample size is a problem in this regression (and mine as well). I am currently seeking to expand the sample size by inviting other anal-compulsive (is this hyphenated or not?) social scientists interested in this phenomenon to join in data collection.

References

Glueck, S. & Glueck, E.T.
Family environment and delinquency
Boston: Houghton Mifflin, 1962

Thompson, Hunter S. (Doctor of Weaponry)
Hell's Angels:
The strange and tenable saga of the outlaw motorcycle gangs
New York: Ballantine Books, 1966

Nod, Emiaa
Multiple Regression with an n of 1
Journal of Very, Very Small Sample Sizes, 1995 (1): 1.01-1.09

Plotinus, J.C.
Sex, Drugs & Rock 'n Roll: What is Rome Coming to?
Proceedings of the Downfall of Civilization As We Know It: X-XX-XXX

"BIPSPISH"

Alistair Munro, M.D., O.C.D.
Halifax, Nova Scotia

Introduction:

All mental health workers are familiar with the problems involved in getting psychiatric patients back to gainful employment, owing to the stigma attached to many conditions, and the prejudices displayed by would-be employers. The **Beacon Institute Placing Square Pegs In Square Holes**, known as BIPSPISH, is a non-profit organization with international campuses dedicated to helping recovering psychiatric patients obtain employment where their talents will be a benefit and their activities thoroughly appreciated.

Background:

The Beacon Institute itself is a long-established charitable body whose name derives from the disorders in which it specializes:

Borderline Personality Disorder
Early **A**lzheimer's Disease
Catatonia
Obsessional Disorder
Narcolepsy

Although it has helped sufferers of other mental conditions, BIPSPISH has found through years of experience that the above are the illnesses for which its methods are particularly well adapted.

Application:

The term Borderline Personality Disorder strikes terror in the hearts of most therapists. The Beacon Institute has identified a vocation whose demands exactly fit the characteristics of these patients. In fact, this placement has been so successful that this profession is now largely staffed by graduates of the program. Consider what happens when you return after a long international flight. You are tired, disheveled, mildly disoriented and anxious lest your smuggled-in wristwatch be discovered. And who is the first person you meet in your home and native land? Your one-and-only local, and very unfriendly, customs officer. That steely-eyed gaze, the ill-concealed sneer of disbelief, the belittling remarks, and the sudden pique when they can't nail you on any charge. Where have you seen this all before? And the beauty of it is, the Beacon Institute doesn't have to expend effort in training these people. They've had what it takes for the job since day one!

Early Alzheimer's Disease can be distressing for patients and their relatives. However, we can now give these people respect and credibility by utilizing the very difficulties presented by their illness: a little forgetfulness, a little uncertainty, a slight tendency to wander off and be delayed in returning, and failure to remember other people's names. Isn't this exactly the description, exactly the picture, of the civil servant you meet over the counter every day when you do business with some branch of the government? It's a shame to have able-bodied people in these jobs when they could be doing something useful, and our patients can do the work equally badly. As well, they usually forget to collect their pay, which helps decrease government spending.

One might think that finding employment for catatonics is a problem, and so it was until the Beacon Institute's Think Tank came up with the ideal answer. Catatonic patients are withdrawn, stuporous, unapproachable, unable to initiate any spontaneous action and have a productivity factor so close to zero it doesn't matter. Any ideas? Hospital middle management! When the Beacon Institute developed this solution it wasted no time in persuading hospitals that it had exactly the right horses for their courses. Hospitals have responded by employing large numbers and have statistics to show that their own cost effectiveness has gone through the recently renovated ceiling. "*Initiate nothing, spend nothing*" has become their motto and they now have a larger group of people not only dedicated to, but designed for, this purpose.

Obsessionals seem easy. Everyone wants a hard-working, punctilious, perfectionistic person on their workforce. Someone who never complains when the boss takes the afternoon off to golf, someone who doesn't want to lead but prefers to follow, quietly mopping up other people's messes as they go along. Such people generally present no employment problems — they are hard at work ensuring that their mildly sociopathic superiors get all the credit without taking any of the trouble. Now, we took the real obsessive-compulsives and can say, with all due modesty, that we triumphed again. High anxiety, preoccupations with moralistic themes, a constant internal struggle with intrusive thoughts expressed in ritual behaviors. At first we thought of the priesthood, particularly because of the high vacancy rates there. But second — and better — thoughts prevailed. Our severe OCDs are now in constant demand everywhere as leaders in the field of Bio-Ethics. They are now paid to confuse everyone with their strangled, constipated, convoluted thinking and at the same time convince everyone that their views on ethics are so ineffably clever that they must be right. Governments everywhere have recognized their ability to reduce health care costs by preventing any worthwhile health care from taking place, and are looking for more.

Lastly, narcolepsy. The niche for these people has only become obvious since universities began to get tough with their promotions and tenure. Instead of occupying a pleasant sinecure for life, professors are now actually having to consider working. But being professors, they find it easier to work at putting other professors down than to do something useful themselves. Thus enter the narcoleptics! BIPSPISH has a register of narcoleptic alumni who are prepared to attend lectures and fall asleep at the drop of a hat, regularly and frequently, singly or together. This is most effective in putting lecturers off their stroke and word soon gets around that Dr. So & So's seminars are soporific in the extreme. Rival teachers are lining up to obtain our services.

It is our hope that this is an adequate outline of the Institute and its aims. We feel we have revolutionized the after-care of long-term psychiatric patients by turning the usual process on its head. We do not see our clients as disabled; they have characteristics which are traditionally considered to be disabling. Our master stroke was to recognize these as entrées to certain occupations which depend on people who display such characteristics.

Do not hesitate to refer your problem to BIPSPISH. And of course, since we are a charitable organization, your tax-refundable contributions will be more than welcome.

• Phone 1-800-BIP-SPISH • Fax 1-800-BEA-CON1

I had been seeing a therapist for about three years . . . .

. . . until I realized I was just hallucinating!

What's Your Line?

Geoffrey Norman
Dorset, Vermont

Sometimes we forget there's an alternative to therapy that's just as effective, and often just as expensive. It's called fishing.

When the editorial-page editor and one of the likely heirs to the throne at the New York Times, Howell Raines, writes a bestseller called *Fly Fishing Through the Midlife Crisis,* it's apparent that some "sea" change in the way we define "therapy" is happening. Of course, over the years, psychoanalysis has had to give up a lot of ground to other therapies, and it seems likely that a lot of them were probably surrogates for what the people in distress really needed in the first place, which was . . . fishing.

There is a certain amount of common ground between angling and analysis. For one thing, there is nothing conclusive about either one. For another, both are expensive. And, for those new to rod and reel, it may be useful to know that there is as much variety of choice available as there is in therapy.

Group Therapy or Party-Boat Fishing

Group therapy is popular because (1) it is cheap, at least relatively, and (2) it provides an opportunity for people to interact with other stiffs and thus counter their feelings of inadequacy. This seems reasonable enough, but there is a fishing alternative. What you do is go down to the dock and book a day on a party boat. Typically, one of these boats will take out from 20 to 100 fishermen for a full day, during which there will be
lots of beer drinking and/or seasickness. And when the action is hot and heavy, and fishermen are sliding in the puke and the slime, tempers can get pretty short and there can be some real good interaction. This can do wonders for the self-esteem — depending on who gets in the first punch.

Freudian Analysis — Atlantic Salmon Fishing

It might cost $50,000 to line up a week's fishing on one of the best rivers at the best time of year, and even then, the water might be low and clear and the salmon may not be in and the angler may not catch anything. The point of his existence will be, to use William Humphrey's phrase, "to cast and cast again." Which sounds a lot like strict Freudian analysis, where the patient talks and talks and the analyst keeps stringing him along.

Gestalt Therapy or Bottom Fishing for Cats

You can have a lot of fun going after channel cats with a cane pole and some chicken guts, but in the end, this is not really the kind of fishing that people mean when they talk about fishing. Similarly, Gestalt, with its complete lack of intellectualizing and preference for rolling around in the mud of emotions, is not the kind of program people think about when they talk about psychiatry.

Jungian Therapy or Steelhead Fishing

Jung taught us to accept the irrationality of the sublime. It is probable that the steelhead fisherman, standing in freezing water up to his nipples, line coiled in his mouth and ice on the corners of his mustache, close to being swept off a rock and drowned but feeling strangely and mysteriously alive, would have been a good contender for Jungian therapy.

Rolfing or Big Game Fishing

Rolfing entails a deep and often painful therapeutic massage during which you are encouraged to cry out in agony, thereby purging yourself of inner demons. Similarly when you are deep water fishing for big game (marlin, swordfish and the like), you are either **a)** bored silly or **b)** in deep physical pain. What you do is troll all day and stare out at the baits while you breathe diesel fumes. If you should hook a marlin, you strap yourself into a chair and strain at the rod until you get a hernia.

And, in the end, you are purified.

Illustrations by Mark Zingarelli

Updated for the 1990's:
Ethical Principles of Psychotherapy

Joel Herscovitch, Ph.D.
London, Ontario

It is **unethical** to:

• Inquire about whether you are in the will of a suicidal patient.

• Refer to impotent patients as "Noodle City."

• Use whoopee cushions on anxious patients.

• Do John Wayne impersonations during a homosexual panic.

• Double bill for obese patients.

• Interpret splitting to Siamese twins.

• Use an ejector button at the end of 50 minutes.

• Interpret missed sessions due to death as resistance.

• Contaminate elegant interpretations with reality.

• Measure lateness in milliseconds to compulsive patients.

• Raise your rates during the bargaining phase of a terminal illness.

• Refer to ECT as a kind of breakdancing.

• Diagnose patients as borderline just because they have more fun than you.

• Arm wrestle over the truth of an interpretation.

• Reply to disclosures of wrong-doing with, "You slimeball."

• Say to a guilt-prone person, "You never call, you never write — *Oy*."

• Use thumbscrews on resistant patients.

• Sneak up on paranoid patients and yell, "Booga-booga."

Ego Psychology Update:
The Transmutation of Ego Defenses

David J. Robinson, M.D.

In his structural theory of the mind, Freud divided the psychic apparatus into the id, the ego and the superego. The ego, being the "middle child" in this arrangement, was set up to get it from both sides. Not only would it have to temper the wildly libidinous urges of the id *and* buffer the harsh prohibitions of the superego, but it would have to do all this while acting as the press agent to the external world. Strategy dictates that a strong offense starts with a strong defense, and Freud appreciated the need for defense mechanisms for the ego, and duly noted repression to be the mother of all defenses. A further cataloguing of ego defenses was provided by his daughter Anna, and Valiant[1] efforts have enumerated still more. Just as Freud's Drive Theory was run over by **Objectionable Relations Theory**[2] and **Selfish Psychology**,[3] ego defenses have had to make adjustments to the multifaceted changes in today's society.

Narcisissy Defenses

Old Defense	New Defense
Primitive Idealization	American Expressization

Explanation: The ultimate expression of "plasticity" — this defense allows the ego to function autonomously from the superego, until the end of the month.

Old Defense	New Defense
Projective Identification	Primate Identification

Explanation: This defense is invoked by over-socialized egos (primarily male) as a way of seeking psychic equilibrium. The imitation of primate behavior is often used in an attempt to achieve this.

Old Defense	New Defense
Distortion	Extortion

Explanation: This is simply distortion relocated to a legal setting.

Old Defense	New Defense
Denial	Alibido

Explanation: This is an amalgamation of two other defenses, *alibi* and *libido*, since the first usually covers the strivings of the second.

Premature Defenses

Old Defense	New Defense
Acting Out	Acting

Explanation: This allows the ego to make the most of the "as if" personality by assuming identities of fictitious characters, often with unusual characteristics. Combined with **relocation**, this can also be a lucrative defense.

Old Defense	New Defense
Regression	Digression

Explanation: The spontaneous use of irrelevant and dated material in a rambling, verbose style assures complacency in others.

Old Defense	New Defense
Passive Aggression	Passé Aggression

Explanation: Here, the ego becomes embroiled in the social milieu and struggles of a prior decade in order to avoid facing the demands of the current one. Some decades (e.g. the sixties) seem heavily favored for this defense.

Old Defense	New Defense
Identification	Incorporation

Explanation: In this defense, an individual's ego is assimilated into that of the corporate image. This is most notably seen in organizations with names abbreviated to three letters, one being an "I" (IBM, CIA, FBI, etc.).

Post-Mature Defenses

Old Defense	New Defense
Controlling	Remote Controlling

Explanation: The ego is able to achieve remarkable control over the external environment with this new defense. Not only is it effective with inanimate objects, but can cause pronounced changes in humans as well.

Old Defense	New Defense
Displacement	Relocation

Explanation: This defense allows the ego to displace itself across municipal, county and federal lines as a way of avoiding confrontation.

Old Defense	New Defense
Isolation	Insulation

Explanation: This is an evolved defense that now gives the ego materials with which to perform the isolating. The use of urea-formaldehyde insulation was one of the early misapplications of this defense.

Victor Mature Defenses

Old Defense   **New Defense**
Humor   Humor

Explanation: No comment.

Old Defense   **New Defense**
Asceticism   Ascorbicism

Explanation: This defense is used in an attempt to undo past abuses with the rabid consumption of vitamins and nutrients (like Ascorbic Acid - Vitamin C) many times above the FDA daily requirement.

Old Defense   **New Defense**
Altruism   Trumanism

Explanation: Plainly stated, this mechanism enables the ego to have hard cash, as well as responsibility, seek a final resting place on one's desk.

Old Defense   **New Defense**
Suppression   Supperession

Explanation: The (usually unilateral) decision to postpone attention to a conscious impulse, at least until after dinner.

References

[1] Valiant, Prince George: The Hierarchical Structure of Ego Defenses
Medieval Psychology; Round Table Press, Sherwood Forest, Nottingham

[2] Maggie, Melanie and Bill
Driven to Detraction: Objectionable Relations Theory
British Schoolboy Publishers; Grate Britain

[3] From Lilliputian to Kohutian:
The Advancement of Self Through Selfish Psychology
Chapter 1: Heinz 57 Manual of Therapeutic Interpretations
Mirror, Mirror on the Wall Press; New York

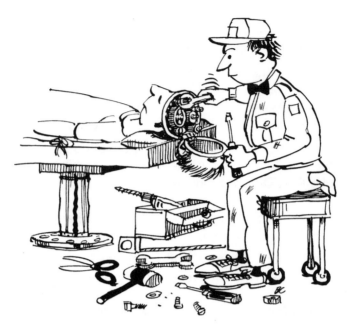

Adjusting the "cogs" in Cognitive Therapy

"Object Relations?"

David J. Robinson, M.D.

Section II
History of Psychiatry & Psychology

Heinz "Comet" Kohutek
Pioneers Selfish Psychology !

David J. Robinson, M.D.

Now Appearing in Your Neighborhood:
Mr. Carl RogersWear™

- Supportive, Warm & Woolly
- Hug and Shrug Resistant
- Knit from the Highest Moral Fiber
- Form Flattering Empathic Fit

RogersWear™

*"Unconditional positive regard for
the genuineness of our guarantee."*

Available at the Client Center Mall

David J. Robinson, M.D.

Benjemil Kranklin

Benjamin Franklin, a founding father
+   Emil Kraepelin, a phenomenal phenomenologist

=   **Benjemil Kranklin**, a flounderer

A flagrant hypochondriac, Kranklin pioneered the field of Psychosomatic Medicine in order to give legitimacy to his wildly varied complaints. He changed the face of Psychiatry (as well as his own) when he unwittingly self-administered ECT during a particularly intense fit of compulsive indignation.

David J. Robinson, M.D.

Was he Wrong or Reich?
Wilhelm Reich

When W.R. set out to query,
Herr Sigmund's sacred theory,
His version of the *Big Bang*,
Used *orgone* for slang,
Without him, cloudbusting has become dreary.

David J. Robinson, M.D.

A Tribute to Albert Ellis:
Rational Expletive Therapy

¶ Hurry Up! I'm on my way to conduct a workshop on overcoming low frustration tolerance, YOU IDIOT !!

¶ Move it YOU GODDAMN ROGERIAN DRIVER !!

¶ You should drive the way I do, YOU IDIOT !!

❣ I obviously run the goddamn universe, GET THE HELL OUT OF MY WAY !!

¶ **by Michael F. Shaughnessy, Ph.D.**   ❣ **by Albert Ellis, Ph.D.**

Rapid Psychler Interviews:
Harry "Smoke-Stack" Sullivan

Psychler: You theorized that when different modes of interaction go awry (protaxic, parataxic and syntaxic), mental illness develops. Can you give us an example?

HSS: Sure, my recent contact with the government is driving me crazy.

Psychler: What mode would that involve?

HSS: Overtaxic, of course.

Psychler: Although you were a firm opponent of Freud, some of your ideas sounded quite similar —

HSS: Where is that little @#$%&* — I'll parataxically distort him!

Psychler: Weren't you as famous for your tantrums as for your theories?

HSS: Listen, you @#$%&*, it takes two to consensually validate that, and until then I'll thank you to keep your opinions to yourself . . .

David J. Robinson, M.D.

At Home on the Primal Anxiety Ranch:
Ottoman Rank

There was a young turk named Rank,
Who thought Freud's theories stank,
Sigmund said he would mourn,
The day he was born,
And his real last name was Krank.

David J. Robinson, M.D.

The Causes of Insanity according to:
Psychiatry in the Good Ol' Daze

Parents

The insane diathesis in the child may come from hysteria in the mother. A drunken father may impel epilepsy, madness or idiocy in the child. Ungoverned passions, from love to hate, from hope to fear, when indulged in overmuch by the parents, may unloose the furies of unrestrained madness in the minds of the children.

Vices

The fast high livers of today are developing, rapidly and surely, strong tendencies to both mental and physical disorders. Elbert Hubbard says, of those who live at a certain hotel and waste their substance there, that they are apt, "to have gout at one end, general paresis at the other, and Bright's Disease in the middle." Drunkenness, lust, rage, fear, mental anxiety or incompatibility, "if admitted to participation in the act of impregnation will each, in turn or in combination, often set the seal of their presence in the shape of idiocy, imbecility, eccentricity or absolute insanity."

Education

Another cause of insanity is forced education in the young. Our present school system tends to break down the body. The work may not be too hard, but the amount of anxiety and worry, which this work causes in the minds of sensitive children, tends to enfeeble them. Many children are sensitive, with nervous temperaments, and they are easily affected by the strain of mental toil. Girls, especially, at the age of puberty, should be built up instead of rushed through a heavy routine of study. Herbert Spencer says, "Go where you will, and before long there comes under your notice cases of children, or youths of either sex, more or less injured by undue study." Here, to recover from a state of debility thus produced, a year's vacation has been found necessary.

Last, But Not Least

Another great cause of insanity is the unnatural, improper and excessive use of the sexual organs . . . I might go on and on and enlarge upon these causes, but enough has been written to give warning to those who are breaking nature's laws.

From the 1920 Medical Text "Mother's Remedies"
by Dr. T. J. Ritter   Submitted by Phyllis Bristow

Excerpts from "Sex as a Sublimation for Tennis"
Selected Case Studies in Tennis Hysteria

Theodor Saretsky, Ph.D.
Hewlett Neck, New York

The quality that distinguishes **Tennis Analysis** from all other forms of treatment is that it is essentially and consciously a very personal form of therapy. No longer is the analyst's role that of a cool, objective observer in an antiseptic atmosphere of clinical neutrality. I choose involved participation in the vicissitudes of the tennis game that is life.

Freud, 1897

Sigmund Freud's open, direct, hands-on approach is best illustrated in his case histories. The following excerpts demonstrate how Freud's understanding of the presenting symptoms from a tennis perspective helped free patients from their psychic suffering.

Case History #1: *The Face of Rage*

Frau Necillie C. suffered from an extremely violent facial neuralgia, appearing suddenly two or three times a year and lasting from five to ten days, that was diagnosed as a guilty self-punishment for wrongful acts. Frau C., being of weak character, frequently grimaced and grounded her serves when her partners made unforced errors; besides that, she had a terrible frown and wince. Because of Frau C.'s good upbringing, the facial symptoms were interpreted as conscience attacks for her inconsiderate behavior.

Dr. Saretsky has written two satirical works:

Sex as a Sublimation for Tennis:
The Secret Writings of Freud (Workman Publishing)

How to Make Your Analyst Love You:
A Guide to Becoming a More Appealing Neurotic (Citadel Press)

Autographed/inscribed copies of these books are available from the author:

Dr. T. Saretsky
1 Madison St.
Hewlett Neck, New York   *Tennis* — $5.95 + $1 postage (U.S. funds)
U.S.A. 11598   *Analyst* — $7.95 + $1 postage (U.S. funds)
                                Prices may vary

Case History #2: *Dora's Dream*

If it is true that the causes of hysterical disorders are to be found in the intimacies of the patients' daily tennis experiences, and that hysterical symptoms are the expression of their most secret and repressed wishes, then the complete elucidation of a case of tennis hysteria involves the revelation of those intimacies and the betrayal of those secrets.

A typical recurring dream is described by Dora:

> "A house was on fire. My father was standing beside
> my bed and woke me up. I dressed quickly. Mother
> wanted to stop and save her two Prince Graphites,
> but Father said, *I refuse to let myself and two children
> be burned for the sake of your tennis rackets.*"

This dream was related to Dora's presenting neurotic symptoms: shortness of breath during the second set, avoidance of men on the court next to her, and a feeling of distress and revulsion whenever a ball lost its fuzz. The dream's latent content — the mother's rejection of Dora for her valuable rackets — was the unconscious basis for her hysterical tantrums every time she tried to play tennis. The suggestion here is that this carrying on only serves as a screen for an unconscious death wish toward the mother, and a denied wish to inherit her rackets. . .

Case History #3: *The Racket Cover & The Raincoat Neurosis*

I will now outline the case of a twenty-seven-year-old man whose libido had been diminished for some time; his preparations for using a condom took hours and were enough to make him feel that the whole act was something forced on him. He spoiled coitus for himself by grossly fearing infection and laying a foundation of alienation from sexual pleasures.

A three-year intensive analysis revealed that this phobic individual had unwittingly been playing tennis without remembering to remove his racket cover. His game had deteriorated considerably as a result, with accompanying symptoms of apathy, dyspepsia and insomnia. Historical reconstruction showed that failure to remove the cover symbolically reflected a childhood defense against exhibitionism and early signs of the "raincoat neurosis."

Excerpts from "Sex as a Sublimation for Tennis"
The Court Is My Couch

Theodor Saretsky, Ph.D.
Hewlett Neck, New York

A great tradition was being established. With Sigmund Freud's encouragement and direction, the original Wednesday Circle, reinforced by apprentice tennis analysts, initiated the dawn of a new age of discovery: the Tennis Instinct Era. Spurred on by Freud's unflagging energy and the stimulus of his latest work, *The Court Is My Couch* (1924), these early zealots tested and reformulated man's tennis destiny in the transparent crucible of the tennis court.*

Until this time, Freud had been naïvely monopolized by his role as a dedicated physician with "the need to cure and to help." Whatever his other beliefs, results from the couch came first. With the evolution of the Tennis Instinct, however, Freud made a fundamental switch in technique. For severely practical reasons, he had always perceived the analyst as an objective outsider listening to his patients' recollections, sifting, sorting, interpreting, but never becoming personally involved. There were, of course, the problems of transference, countertransference and yawning, but these were minor problems and could be dealt with through care, common sense and discipline.

> * Freud's famous tennis case studies are pure works of art. Who wili
> ever forget the String Man, Hanna O., the Net Man, Little Hands,
> the Racketeer and the Wolf Man? This extraordinary assemblage
> of detached clinical observations preserved for posterity the living
> drama of Tennis Psychoanalysis.

Now Freud adopted the more daring approach that lack of parental love, manifesting itself through ambivalence toward the children's overtures with regard to playing tennis, lay at the root of much mental anguish. This could be remedied and compensated for if the analyst modified his technique and assumed a more personal attitude toward his patients. Slowly, Freud's own basic tenets gave way to his burgeoning interest in the details of each patient's tennis background: the deprivations and trauma he suffered; the various rackets he used, as well as how they were strung and the pressures they were under; where he bought his equipment; the tennis outfits he wore; who he played with and what he felt when he played. Finally Freud took the great leap forward when he stated categorically that, "The only way to know one's patients is to play tennis with them."

Great work followed upon great work in an incredible display of virtuosity: *Fuzzy Balls and Pubic Hair, Flakiness on the Tennis Court* (or, *The Mental Anguish of Dandruff*); *Enjoying Your Mis-hits: The Power of Negative Thinking; Civilized Tennis Morality* and *Modern Nervousness.*

The seriousness with which Freud viewed these concepts is best illustrated by his sober reminder, two years before his death, that "the awesome healing power of the Tennis Unbewusstsein (Tennis Unconsciousness) is man's best answer to the death instinct" (in *The Nightmare of the Canceled Tennis Game: A Study in Obesity, Perversion and Suicide*).

His final known work, *The Reach Should Not Exceed the Grasp* (1938), is so complex, so multilayered, that it remains for future generations of scholars to unearth its hidden meaning.

To these scholars, Freud's semimystical statements deriving directly from Tennis Instinct Theory offer fresh hope and certainly a more interesting response to human suffering than the tired, empty enticements of sexuality. (As Freud wisely observed about the act of intercourse, "Once you've had it, what do you have?"). His hypotheses are enduring, classic contributions, seeds of the long-awaited general model of human behavior.

While on the surface tennis may seem to be merely another sport, Freud suggests that its creation was above all a means to an end: "The very structure of the game opens possibilities to human insights and understandings that previously would have been impossible." (1934).

Tennis, to Freud, represented a vehicle for self-expression, a broad screen upon which life can be projected in infinite detail: "In modern times I identify tennis as a cathartic outlet that is most necessary not only for the understanding but for the survival of the species.*

The putrefaction and decay of sexual interest and the problems that go with it have undoubtedly hastened the development and emergence of the Tennis Urge" (1932). For Freud, tennis was the metaphor of our time.

* Six chronically compulsive lobbers were spared the harsh option of banishment from their tennis club or involuntary lobotomy as a result of a more humane interpretation of their antisocial behavior.

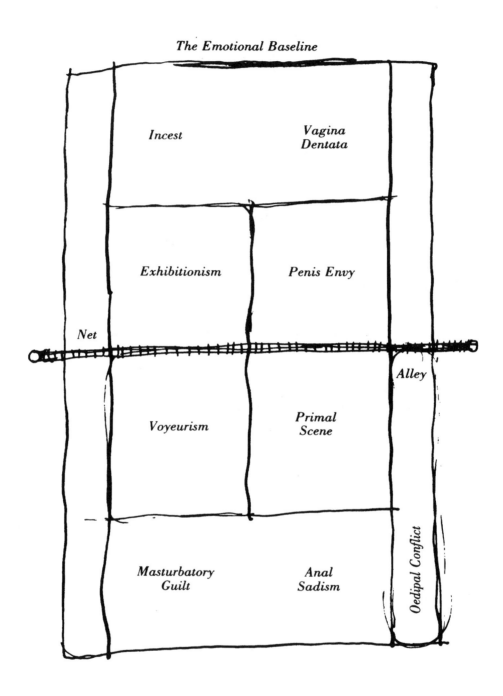

The tennis court in psychological terms, rendered by
an unknown artist from Freud's personal description.

Section III
Political Commentary

The Therapist as Provider-Survivor

David J. Robinson, M.D.

Abstract

In many facets of society, being *politically correct* involves a change in vocabulary. Mental health care recipients have been termed "consumers" and more recently "consumer-survivors." The Random House College Dictionary Revised Edition defines the verb **consume** as, "to destroy or expend by use; to destroy as by decomposition or burning; to undergo destruction." This article identifies the therapist as the material object undergoing consumption and proposes that the politically correct term should be changed to provider-survivor.

Method

Therapists at a "small mid-western college" were contacted via bulk mail and offered a free pizza and beer coupon in exchange for completing the survey. Those who didn't respond were sought out after-hours at such diverse locations as bingo parlors and garage sales. Participants were asked to outline their reactions to job stress, especially in dealing with consumer-survivors who didn't conform to their theoretical orientation. The results were tabulated using the **All-inclusive Psychopathology Assessment (APA).**

Results

The APA instrument organized stress-related effects into categories, which were then listed in declining frequency of respondents experiencing the particular symptom or activity.

Regressive Behavior

- Lampooning One's Profession (writing or reading such literature)
- Adopting Patient Characteristics (imitating walk, borrowing neologisms)
- Sleepwalking (entering the wrong house to raid a neighbor's fridge)
- Bedwetting (includes spilling drinks while recumbent)
- Work Refusal (*magical thinking* regarding current work circumstances)

Oral Dependency

- Fast Food (talks in *burgerspeak*, sees income in burger potential)
- Beverages (Johnnie Walker appears on the guest list at social events)
- Tobacco (includes cigars, chewing tobacco and corn-cob pipes)
- Inanimate Objects (chews nails, co-workers' pens, soothers)
- Non-Beverage Alcohol (applying gauche amounts of cologne/perfume)

Antisocial Activities
- Retreating into Trendy Business Literature (prepares a battle plan for the next session based on Ancient Japanese swordsmanship)
- Layering of Ego Defenses (*denial* of r*ationalization*)
- Over-Investment in Technology (pioneers a computer-based therapy program)
- Cinema Therapy (finds a movie metaphor to illustrate pathology to friends)
- Institutionalization (places children and pets on behavioral programs)

Discussion
Compared to the "consumer-survivor" (C/S), the "provider-survivor" (P/S) seems to be more affected by therapeutic interactions. C/S's at least appear to have spells of relatively normal functioning which are interspersed with periods of psychosis or neurosis. According to this survey, P/S's are not afforded this benefit, which is not surprising considering the time factor involved. C/S's are involved in therapy, at most, a few hours per week generally dealing with the same problems. P/S's, on the other hand, are involved for a minimum of 40 hours per week in continually varying situations and may be confined to an institution until retirement.

The impact of this considerably bleaker situation is reflected in the high percentage of therapists reporting difficulties on the APA scale. No single P/S was free of all the symptoms listed, and over half fulfilled criteria from all three categories. Many P/S's reported themselves as also being consumers.

Comment
The overriding concern related to these findings stems from the Random House definition of the verb **survive**, which is "to remain alive after the death of another, or in spite of a mortally dangerous occurrence or situation; one of two persons having a joint interest who outlives the other." This raises the possibility that an amalgamated "Provider-Consumer" entity may yet emerge, but cause its own extinction when therapy is sought.

References
I.M. Nitro & U.R. Glycerin: "A Disastrous Case of Consumer/Provider Survivalism"
Journal of Therapeutic Conflicts: TNT Press; Big Bang, Texas

M.T. Head & P. Brain: "Increasing Policy Making Decision Power as a Function of Increasing Distance from the Actual Delivery of Health Care" from, *The Little Red Book of Health Care*
Cerebral Castration Publishers: Snippy, South Carolina

Managed Ethics

Mitchell Handelsman, Ph.D.
Denver, Colorado

In the old days, psychologists were taught that clients and patients were worthy of respect (actually, clients were a bit more worthy than patients, but that's beside the point now). This respect led to a multitude of ethical obligations, including confidentiality, informed consent, the obligation to put a happy face on reminders about unpaid bills, etc. However, managed care has necessitated managed ethics; we can no longer afford to dispense dignity in large doses as if there were enough to go around to everyone who thought they deserved it.

I am starting my own managed ethics company, called E-M-D-R (not to be confused with EMDR, with which it has no connection). This stands for "**E**thics **M**anagement and **D**ignity **R**ationing." Naturally I cannot divulge all the particulars of my business; this is proprietary information! But I can give you some background. As was covered extensively on *A Current Affair*, Oregon recently implemented a health-care rationing plan. All medical procedures were rated by a blue-ribbon panel in terms of their efficacy, necessity, and the number of syllables in the name of the procedure.

In a similar way, ethics management organizations have put together blue smiley-faced panels of psychologists (called the **EMDr**, or "Everything-Might-Decompensate-rapidly" panel) who have rated professional obligations in a similar manner. For example, they found that boundaries have been terribly over-utilized. Based on the work of this panel, E-M-D-R and other managed ethics organizations have replaced the long, comprehensive list of ethical obligations with "Preferred Professional Obligations" (P.P.O.s). There are only a limited number of ethical principles that can be on this list at any one time. If clients would like additional rights such as more information about risks or advance financial arrangements, they have to pay extra. Likewise, if they would like their information kept confidential for more than ten sessions, they have to petition their Ethics Managers for an extension (I hear they're hard to get).

As you can see, this is NOT a capitated system; rather, it is a **decapitated** system — with no head being involved at all!

Where will Ethics Managers come from? From my intensive program, called **EMdR** (for "Ethics Means doing Right") training. Students in this program will need at least a sixth grade education and evidence of potentially making it into Kohlberg's third level of ethical reasoning. The coursework consists of intensive study and reworking of classic ethical problems. For example, instead of Heinz stealing the drug to save his wife, he will enter psychotherapy, file for divorce, and then sue for custody of the pharmacist.

Graduates of the **EMdR** academy will earn an **EmDR** ("Entirely moral & Definitely Righteous") certificate, and will be paid at a rate of 104.5% of the average therapist salary. Encouragingly, training takes only a few days.

If you would like to join E-M-D-R, please send a check or money order for a third of your projected client fees over the next three years (or the number of different insurance forms you will fill out over that time, whichever is larger) to the **eMDR** Foundation (that's "even Mitch Deserves to Retire" Foundation). So you don't forget, send it before midnight tomorrow.

A version of this article appeared in the **Colorado Psychological Association Bulletin** in February, 1996 — but nobody reads it.

                                        M.H.

State of the Art Mental Health Care Reform:
Putting Money First — A Capital Idea

David J. Robinson, M.D.

Introduction
It used to be that medicine was considered a calling, not a trade. Therapists were able to focus attention on improving the quality of life for those in their practice. This allowed the remainder of the population to devote their attention to improving the quality of the small pieces of colored paper in their lives. This often struck therapists as unfortunate, because the pieces of paper themselves were not that unhappy. The current state of mental health funding indicates that the traditional approach needs to be updated. Therapists now need to join the rest of society and give direct attention to the small colored pieces of paper.

Method
The practices of Psychiatry, Psychology, Social Work and Rehabilitative Medicine have developed light years beyond what was available when most dignitaries were emblazoned on currency. A comprehensive assessment and treatment plan for these individuals would no doubt improve their situation.

Case Examples
U.S. $50 — ULYSSES S. GRANT
Ulysses S. Grant, born Hiram Ulysses Grant, changed his name in order to avoid his initials spelling H.U.G., which is unfortunate because he could use one. He is a very heavy smoker and drinker, and as an old soldier clearly could use some exercise — like marching through some 12-step programs. He needs vocational rehabilitation because up until the time of the Civil War he failed at every job he attempted. Lastly, a dietary consultation would encourage him to improve on his favorite breakfast of cucumber soaked in vinegar.

U.S. $1000 — GROVER CLEVELAND
Grover is the second heaviest president to ever serve in office and duly earned the nickname "Uncle Jumbo." He gave early credence to the hereditary theory of obesity when the "Baby Ruth" chocolate bar was named for his daughter. A behavioral modification program and reducing diet are clearly in order. Leisure counseling is also indicated, as he refused to admit the State of Hawaii to the Union.

U.S. $20 — ANDREW JACKSON
Andrew Jackson, a rough and ready sort, has the nickname "Old Hickory" as much for his toughness as for the way he smells. Not only did he order spittoons for the White House, but he single-handedly subdued the first would-be presidential assassin with his own cane. He is badly in need of pharmaco-therapy for his Intermittent Explosive Disorder. Additionally, with the wildest and most destructive inauguration on record, he and his gang need psychotherapy for their Group Type Conduct Disorder.

CANADIAN $10 — SIR JOHN A. MACDONALD
Sir John has been known to tip the bottle on more than a few special occasions. He and his crapulent clan went on a cross-country bender that resulted in them being ordained as the Confabulating Fathers of Confederation. A 28-day residential program would suit Sir John nicely. His wife describes him as having pronounced mood swings, thus a mood stabilizer would help even out his manic sprees and depressive frugality. When visiting England to wrest the Dominion of Canada from the Monarchy, he and his merry band shot at the British public with peashooters. Accordingly, an interpretation of the Oedipus Complex would benefit him.

CANADIAN $50 — WILLIAM LYON MACKENZIE KING
King, who conducts séances, regularly speaks to the dead, and feels he is guided directly by God, could clearly be helped by an antipsychotic. He remains unmarried, and counts as his only friends the British mediums who conduct his séances and a series of terriers all named Pat. Social Skills Training would enable him to interact with others in a more appropriate way. He is also a muddler of almost supernatural skill, and would be helped considerably by Assertiveness Training.

CANADIAN $100 — ROBERT BORDEN
Robert Borden, a classic Type A workaholic, is a one-ulcer man holding down a four-ulcer job. His vain efforts in cycling to work do not compensate for his compulsive tobacco chewing. He complains of lumbago, neuritis and sciatica and clearly needs help for his Somatization Disorder. He switched political alliances early in his career to spite his family, and group therapy could help him temper his rebellious instincts.

Comment
The immediate introduction of the various therapeutic modalities listed here is sorely needed. It is hoped that once on the road to recovery, the small colored pieces of paper will once again exhibit their previous vitality and resume circulation thereby making everyone happy.

Community Care Center Psychiatry (CCCP)

ONE CORPORATE CIRCLE
FORT KNOX, KY $$$$$-$$$$

Friday the 13th

To: Administrators
Medical Staff
All CCCP Psychiatric Hospitals

From: Corporate Central Coordinators of Programming

Re: **Voo-Doo Psychiatry Units**

This is to announce that as of this date, we are establishing Voo-Doo psychiatry units in all company facilities, nationwide. The prototype unit, the *Marie Leveau Institute of Transsphere Psychiatry* at the (New Orleans) Crescent City Center for Psychiatry has been very successful. We believe that we are filling a void, so to speak, in the market.

A battalion of Psychiatric Palmists and Entrails Technicians has recently completed rigorous training programs at Corporate Headquarters, and the trainees will assume their individual local assignments in time to provide in-service training to all hospital and medical staff. Programs will be well established before the planned *Hallowe'en Open House Séance Therapy Marathons* (Administrators see attached *Press Releases*).

You will all be very pleased to know that the ghost of Dr. Wilheim Reich has agreed to accept the position as Director of all the units, thus filling three full-time EPOB's (24-hr duty) for each unit, *at no cost to CCCP!* Orgone boxes will be centrally placed at each Nursing Station to provide ready access to Dr. Reich. It is only fair that we inform you that some screams have been reported from the ghost of a "Dr. Janov." As of this writing, we are offering him a consulting staff contract, and he will also be assigned to the Board of Trustees of all facilities. For those concerned that your input has not been solicited in the planning of this project, we can only say that our mediums have induced manifestations of each employee at every project planning conference and board meeting where this project has been discussed. We are very grateful that everyone contributed so constructively in this effort to advance the science of psychiatry.

Please feel free to begin referring patients to the following new programs:

- Tea Leaf Diagnostic Sit-ins
- Astrology Groups
- Crystal Therapy Channeling
- Tarot Card Blackjack
- Aromatherapy Sneeze-Offs
- Daily reruns of *Ghost*
- Séances

There are plans for outpatient Telepathy Groups as part of the aftercare program. As this develops into a regular program, future memos will not be required.

If the Telepathy Group is successful, there are tentative plans to enhance this service and simultaneously move it into the high-tech arena by marketing a PC software package that facilitates the telepathic process. Beginners may use modems, of course, but mastery of the process will render this cumbersome hardware item entirely redundant. The program is called, "OM_in.exe" and is available at $895.00 (copy protected) from CCCP Software, Inc.

Negotiations are underway for Medicare reimbursement.

If you have comments or questions, you need only meditate —
our mediums will find you out there, somewhere.

---

by Lawrence D. Wade, M.D.
Baton Rouge, Louisiana

The Rapid Psychler Solution:
Irrationalizing Mental Health Care

David J. Robinson, M.D.

The relentless cuts to funds for research, social services and in some cases professional fees known as "health care reform" make it increasingly difficult to maintain our high standards of care. Canada represents a paradigm of this problem due to its extremely large area, small population and cultural diversity. In order to more effectively deploy health care services, Rapid Psychler has devised a geographic solution for mental health care. Duplication of services can be avoided by

relocating patients to places that specialize in treating a particular condition. In order to avoid the logistical nightmare of naming treatment centers, existing locations will be used. The following is a list of authorized treatment centers:

Diagnosis
MOOD DISORDERS

Location

Manic Phase	Apex Hill, NWT
	Ha! Ha!, PQ; Ha Ha, NF
	Happyland Creek, SK
	Mount Indefatigable, AB
	Mount Invincible, AB
	Rapid City, MB
	Zealand, ON
Depressed Phase	Disappointment River, NWT
	Helluva Hole, NS
	Downie Island, ON
	Purgatory Glacier, BC
	Hanging Heart Lake, AB
	Pitt Island, BC

Diagnosis	Location
MOOD DISORDERS CONTINUED	
Vegetative Signs	Peas Brook, NS; Carrot River, SK Potato Creek, YT; Leek Island, ON Spud Island (nickname for PEI)
Unresponsive to Prozac	Anzac, AB & BC
ANXIETY DISORDERS	
Generalized Anxiety	Distress, NF Squamish, BC
Obsessive-Compulsive	Kemptville, ON
Posttraumatic Stress	Alert, NWT
SUBSTANCE ABUSE	
Alcohol	Devil's Punch Bowl, MB Pocomoonshine Deadwater, NB Brandy Brook, NB
Narcotics	Mount Nirvana, NWT Paradise, NS & NF
Tobacco	Mount Bogart, AB
Marijuana	Air Line Junction, ON
EATING DISORDERS	
Anorexia Nervosa	Famish Gut, NF Dinner Place Creek, MB Devil's Kitchen, NFLD
Bulimia Nervosa	Lac des Bonbons, PQ Chocolate Cove, NB Coffee Creek, ON Canmore, AB Dumpling Savannah, NS Devil's Cupboard, NS

Key to provinces and territories:
AB — Alberta, BC — British Columbia, MB — Manitoba, ON — Ontario
NB — New Brunswick, NF — Newfoundland, NS — Nova Scotia
NWT — Northwest Territories, PEI — Prince Edward Island
PQ — Quebec, SK — Saskatchewan, YT — Yukon Territory

Diagnosis   ## Location
PERSONALITY DISORDERS

Antisocial

Bastard Township, ON
Mount Beelzebub, BC
Bloodletter Island, ON
Mount Black Prince, AB
Bow and Arrow Shoal, NFLD

Borderline

Cape Split, NS
Ogre Mountain, BC

Dependent

Buttermilk Creek, NB
Closeleigh, YT

Histrionic

Avondale, ON; Avonmore, ON
Mount Cupid, ON; Eros Lake, ON
Hickey Island, ON; Lac Kiss, PQ
Lover's Lane, ON; Valentine, ON
Mount Romeo, BC; Mount Juliet, BC
Lac de l'Amour, PQ

Narcissistic

King City, ON; Queen Peak, BC
Upper Canada Village, ON
Admirality Islands, ON
Star City, SK

Obsessive-Compulsive

Penny Ice Cap, NWT
Nickel Belt, ON; Resolute, NWT

Paranoid

Secret Creek, YT

Passive-Aggressive

Bury Head, PEI
Snafu¶ Creek, YT
Tarfu* Creek, YT

Schizoid

Lac Onoman, PQ

Schizotypal

Mount DeCosmos, BC
Witch Spirit Lake, BC
Sorcerer Mountain, BC

¶ Situation Normal — All Fouled Up
* Things Are Really Fouled Up

Diagnosis	Location

SOMATOFORM DISORDERS

Somatization Disorder — Gastown, BC; Gasburg, AB
Devil's Thumb, AB & BC
Fiddler's Elbow, ON; Yahk, BC
Pinchgut Tickle, NFLD

Pain Disorder — Backside of Hell Cove, NFLD
Devil's Rectum, BC

DELUSIONAL DISORDERS

Favorable Content — Bay of God's Mercy, NWT
Garden of Eden, ON & NS
God's Lake, MB
Little Heaven Island, ON

Unfavorable Content — Hades Islands, ON
Devil's Warehouse Island, ON

Somatic Content — Devil's Limb, NS; Devil's Hand, NB
Devil's Tongue, BC; Devil's Tooth, BC
Devil's Elbow, YT

Nihilistic Content — Dead Man's Flat, AB
Deathdealer Island, ON

SEXUAL DISORDERS — Crotch Lake, ON
Great Slave Lake, NWT

MARITAL DISCORD — International Rift, ON
Meetinghouse Rips, NB

After Conflict Resolution — Harmony Mills, NS
Little Heart's Ease, NFLD
New Harmony, PEI
Peace River, AB
Utopia Lake, BC & NB
Valhalla, AB & MB

References
Alan Rayburn
Naming Canada: Stories about Place Names from Canadian Geographic
University of Toronto Press; Toronto, Canada, 1994

That Was Then, This Is Now

Morton S. Rapp, M.D.
Toronto, Ontario

I don't want to give the impression that I have trouble throwing things away. But while I was rummaging through some papers the other day, I found a clipping dated Friday April 19, 1963. It concerned a psychiatrist who refused to testify with regard to interviews he had had with a patient. A Dr. William Peter Kyne risked being jailed for contempt of court, because he felt his patient's confidences should be protected. Mr. Justice C.D. Stewart told Dr. Kyne that he could jail him for "contempt," but refused to do so. Some of Mr. Justice Stewart's comments are worth repeating here.

He told Dr. Kyne that confidences between patient and doctor are not privileged, but that he himself found it "shocking" that this was so, and would refuse to punish Dr. Kyne. "It is the genius of the common law to move with the time," he said. "When the law was first promulgated, there was no such thing as a psychiatrist; a surgeon was a barber, and a physician was little more than a herbalist. Today the situation is quite otherwise." He found it "shocking to the conscience" that statements made under the impression that they were in confidence could later be given out in public. He further found it shocking that one profession (law) could dictate to another (medicine) in these matters.

Well, as the politicians are so fond of saying when they reverse themselves by 180 degrees, "That was then and this is now." So I created what I thought would be a typical judge's response to any psychiatrist who tried the same thing today.

. . . .

"You worm (Pronounced woooorm)! How dare you presume to think that your confidences should be kept? How dare you think that you can stand in the way of lawyers making money? How can you stand there and presume that your work is of any importance whatsoever?"

"Who do you think you are? God? Well, let me tell you that in this court, I am God! Moi! Not toi! You are here because your closely guarded secrets will be of financial value to decent litigants and of great titillation value to the local newspapers!"

"You wish to stand there and represent the de-spi-sed (3 syllables) profession of medicine? Whom do you think you are deceiving? You are a public servant. You will do as you are commanded by me, by the lawyers, by the Ministry of Truth, by anyone who wants you to jump through whatever hoop, in their pursuit of financial gain and salve to the ego. And furthermore, you will smile as you do it!"

"*Why* should the smarmy little secrets revealed during your so-called *treatment* not be grist for the legal mill? It isn't as if you were someone important like a herbalist, say, or a hairdresser. Now a hairdresser has got to keep secrets. I can relate to that!"

"I suppose you will plead that you forgot to tell your patient that so-called confidences placed with you were more or less public property? You forgot to tell him about the Highway Traffic Act, the Worker's Compensation Act, Bill 100, Bill 50 and any number of other laws which make it unnecessary for us to use electronic eavesdropping, because we can use you instead? You forgot to mention this, did you?"

"Off to jail with you. And by the time you get to stand in front of the Licensing Board, I swear there won't be enough left of you to mount a defense."

"Oh incidentally (as the doctor is being dragged off to jail by the thumbs), my daughter is depressed and wishes to see you. Could you arrange it for say, next Saturday at 10:00 am, which would be most convenient. And don't say a word about this to anyone. Next case!"

. . . .

My how the imagination does run wild while cleaning out old papers.
Such fantasy! Such hyperbole!

Fight Didn't Work:
Fright or Flight From City Hall?

Morton Rapp, M.D.
Toronto, Ontario

For several years, Ontario physicians have been enjoying a toboggan ride down the slippery slope of government-controlled health care. Socialized medicine saw the introduction of a fee schedule with set amounts that the provincial government was prepared to pay for physicians' services. Until 1986, doctors were allowed to charge in excess of this schedule and collect this directly from patients. The government party that stopped this practice was so unpopular that when their leader entered a contest to appear on Canada's $1 coin, he lost to the common loon. When they were soundly defeated, the whole province rejoiced and went on a three-day drunk, waking to cries of, "We elected who?" In contrast to the millions who later denied voting for them, the perennial underdog socialist party won. As a policy, this government systematically alienated every major professional organization. Doctors were affected when an arbitrary ceiling was put on health care expenditures, with the overage deducted from physicians' pay **after** services had been rendered. The author presents a collection of his correspondence with the Ministry of Orwell during the reign of the dark side of the force.

GOVERNMENT OF ONTARIO
MINISTRY OF HEALTH

January 31, 1991

Dear Doctor:

Thank you for your account remittance of Jan. 1989. Your claims will be processed in our usual speedy manner. Because of difficulties in meeting the payroll, your next cheque will be subject to a small roll-back of 2%. This will permit the implementation of several important health-care initiatives, such as the Ontario-Japan Trade Mission.

Sincerely,

A. Fascist

P.S. In answer to your inquiry, the roll-back has nothing to do with egg-rolls, which are of Chinese origin. We are surprised at your lack of erudition.

GOVERNMENT OF ONTARIO
MINISTRY OF HEALTH

April 5, 1991

Dear Team Player in the Newly Reformed Medical
Enterprise:

The Ministry was delighted to receive your claim, and notes with satisfaction
that the recently introduced roll-back of 2% has not significantly altered your
life-style. Starting the in near future (after my coffee break, in fact) all
remittances payable to you will be subject to a hold-back of 2.78888%, a
figure agreed upon through the usual form of free and easy negotiation with
your professional body. We released the President's children the moment he
signed the Memorandum of Understanding (he now understands). Monies
accrued will be used to erect a new Worker's Compensation Building, which
is necessary to ensure that workers do not get compensated.

Sincerely,

B. Brother

P.S. No, there can be no hold-back on the roll-back.

GOVERNMENT OF ONTARIO
MINISTRY OF HEALTH

May 7, 1992

Dear Health Care Conscript:

The Government wishes to point out to you that the jagged rips and tears
you are noticing on your lab-coat are due to our recent claw-back of
4.0006%. We are sorry that the claws proved to have such sharp talons, and
have referred to problem to an aviarist. We are sure you have a clear
understanding of the roll-back, the hold-back and the claw-back, because
we have not received any letters of complaint from your ilk; or if we have, we
have misplaced them. Additionally we've been funding a public awareness
campaign with part of the money we've kept.

Sincerely,

Ruth Less

P.S. How is the soup at the shelter? Hot, we hope.

GOVERNMENT OF ONTARIO
MINISTRY OF HEALTH

March 7, 1993

Dear Politically Disadvantaged:

Thank you for your recent claims submission, but why do you bother? For each one you send, you know we are going to create another reason for reducing your remittance. How else can the government (may it endure a thousand conservative caucuses) pay for all those provincial consultants?

Incidentally, we have switched software from IBM to Macintosh, and have had to raise our processing fee to $2.94 per claim. Just send the money directly to Bob Macintosh, creator of the software and brother-in-law to You'd Never Guess Who.

Sincerely,

W. E. Rule

GOVERNMENT OF ONTARIO
MINISTRY OF HEALTH

May 7, 1994

Dear Property:

The Ministry views with disdain your suggestion that the Government (blessed be its name) will not respond to your reasonable requests for information. Regarding your question about the current amounts of roll-back, hold-back and claw-back, we wish to inform you that these matters are under the Freedom of Information Act, which is designed to ensure that you receive no information — and certainly not for free. The fee for this is $5,000 (U.S. funds, please) and a properly signed form 233B, and we will provide the information.

Sincerely,

Y. R. Nemesis

P.S. You were enquiring about the existence of a so-called "quarterback." We are delighted to reply. After your fee submission is subjected to the roll-back, the hold-back and the claw-back, a "quarterback" is all you get.

Section IV
Pharmacotherapy

Just what is *your* interpretation of "take exactly as directed?"

Bitcheril®

Oliver Robinow, M.D.
Vancouver, BC

BITCHERIL: *tri-caffeinated-primadonna-adnauseate-turbobitchin-hydrazine*
A proprietary brand attitude suppressant for hospital-based, private-practice and academic psychiatrists.

Supplied as
• Bitcheril™ Regular Strength — 250mg tablets
• Bitcheril™ Extra Strength — 500mg tablets
• Bitcheril™ STAT — 750mg IM Blow Dart Form
• Bitcheril™ PMS — 5g long acting IM form - once monthly injection
• Bitcheril™ EverFlow — 50 g/L IV formulation

Indications
For the reduction of attitude, grandiosity and pomposity in formal or informal settings; alleviates feelings of superiority and rampant indignation.

Action
Temporarily deadens attitudinal receptors in the superior portion of the locus narcissisticus in the dominant frontal lobe.

Dosage
Note: these are guidelines only; dosages can be increased in cases of exceptional attitude or treatment resistance.

Psychotherapists: 2 tablets per 50-minute hour; may be increased to 2 extra-strength tablets if symptoms persist.

Psychopharmacologists: Required dosage of 5000 mg per hour makes oral administration impractical; generally continuous intravenous infusion is required.

Researchers: During routine research generally require monthly injection; while writing research proposals Blow Dart AND one of the Alternate Forms (on next page) are required.

Malignant Eclectasists: Research has shown attitudinal receptors in this group are immune to suppression. No formulation has shown any efficacy.

Possible Side Effects

Mental
- confusion (often worse in the morning)
- daytime somnolence (often worse later in the day)
- cerebral rigidity (may be age related)

Verbal
- repetitive affirmative grunting
- use of bland or generic interpretations
- compulsion to rephrase others' words

Behavioral
- chronic watch checking
- chin rubbing
- head bobbing

Other
- sporadic facial hirsutism
- tendency to dress and conceptualize in shades of gray
- rabid consumption of caffeinated beverages

Alternate Forms

WhineAway®
A mild attitude suppressant in a pleasant-tasting cappuccino-flavored liquid form for those who can't stop talking long enough to take the tablets. Also practical for surreptitious introduction into colleagues' coffee mugs.

Nag-B-Gone®
Bitcheril strength attitude suppressant in an aerosol form with two settings:
- wide setting works as an antiperspirant
- narrow setting delivers an effective dose across conference rooms.

Flock-Off®
A triple-strength formulation available in suppository form. For use in extreme cases, such as meetings composed of multitudes of the individuals listed above.

Narciss-Fix-All®
An experimental community-based formulation suitable for inclusion in water supply; government approval is pending for endemic areas.

Pharmaco-Acronym-Mania

David J. Robinson, M.D.

Have you ever wondered where drug names come from? How come there aren't any fun names for psychiatric drugs, such as **Duvoid** for urinary hesitancy, or **Fastin**, an anorexiant? Why can't we have **HallucinHalten** as an anti-psychotic, or **WorryBuster** for an anxiolytic? Or could it be that there are *subliminal* messages contained in the names of these medications . . .

Librium	**Lib**erally given to r**um**mies
Haldol	**Ha**d last **d**isagreement with **o**rderly
Largactil	**Larg**ely **act**ing on **i**mpulse
Modecate	**Mod**ulate **cat**atonic symptoms **e**asily
Imap	**I**njectable **ma**nagement **p**rogram
Orap	**Ora**l **p**acification
Prozac	**Pro**motes **z**est and **ac**tivity
Mellaril	**Mell**owed out **a**nd **r**esting at **l**ast
Serentil	**Seren**e un**til** dawn
Ativan	**A**n**ti**cipation **van**quishes me
Halcion	**Halc**yon "daze" **i**sn't **o**nly **n**ostalgia
Anafranil	**A**m **n**ot **afra**id of **n**ew pi**ll**s
Marplan	**M**.D.'s **a**lternate **plan**
Elavil	**Ela**tion and **vi**tality
Dartal	**Dar**n i**t** **w**asn't long-acting
Zoloft	**Z**enith **of loft**y heights
Risperdal	**Ris**k of relapse **per**ishe**d al**together
Effexor	**Effe**ctive in **x**en**o**phobia **r**eduction

Section V
Academia, Reports & Education

The Generic Recursive Epistobabble Generator (G.R.E.G.)*

William H. Watson, Ph.D.
Rochester, New York

Reading too many articles on constructivism, aesthetics, or paralinguistic narrative semiotics, the way many of them are written these days, can put one at risk for developing intellectual vertigo. Language in these articles is often characterized by an absence of referents to the actual world of therapy (or, some may say, to most anything else). One can be left feeling quite at sea about what exactly the point is, where reality is, or what's for dinner (depending, of course, on whether dinner *really* exists or exists merely in language). This linguistic ambiguity was nicely captured and lampooned by Coyne[§] who playfully coined the term "epistobabble" to describe this new way of speaking. It was in the spirit of creative confusion bred by drinking deeply from the wellsprings of these contemporary philosophies that the following device presented itself. It is offered here for those unfortunates among us who feel left out at seminars, cocktail parties, or other gatherings where these theories are being knowledgeably discussed. Fear not, and apologize no more! Now with G.R.E.G. tucked in pocket or purse (or cheek), you too can confidently assert, "*From a cybernetic viewpoint, homeostatically purposive networks inevitably lead to diagnostically-based meaning systems. On the other hand, metaphysical contextual errors often occur when ignoring Bateson's idea that abductive antithetical abstractions virtually always induce polyocular linguistic-kinesthetic muddles.*" Sure, no one will have the vaguest notion what you have said, but no one will dare question you. They will simply nod knowingly, secretly envious of the remarkable grasp you have of family therapy's most esoteric mysteries.

Operating Instructions

In order to produce quality epistobabble with a minimum of fuss, muss or epistomologic error, simply choose one phrase from Section I, another from Section II, a verb-like phrase from Section III, and in a cybernetic recursive fashion, close with a phrase from Section IV. Compile several paragraphs to amaze your friends, astound your colleagues, and confuse your students.

* From the **Journal of Marital and Family Therapy**, p.187-88, April 1991 Reprinted with permission.
§ J. C. Coyne: A Brief Introduction to Epistobabble, **Family Therapy Networker** (6), p. 27-8, 1982

Section I
- Bateson maintained that
- From a cybernetic viewpoint
- Syllogisms deduced from
- Bateson *actually* felt that
- Patterns that connect
- According to Maturana's agreement with Bateson,
- Varela often secretly thought that
- Maruyama, not to be confused with Maturana, reflects that
- Bateson himself *repeatedly* asserted, without fear of contradiction, that
- As Bateson's cleaning lady viewed them
- A quantum mechanic's
- Quasilinear vibrating orbs with
- Multiple versions of
- Self-contained unteachable autopoets gently suggest that
- Metaphysical contextual errors often occur when ignoring Bateson's idea that

Section II
- diagnostically-based meaning systems
- abductive antithetical abstractions
- fundamental pragmatic determinisms
- homeostatically purposive networks
- paradoxical ecological epistemologies
- epistemic partial lobotomies
- aesthetically-based pragmatists
- pragmatically-faced anesthetists
- decontextualized holistic cybernetics
- simultaneous dialectical explosions
- holistic resonating part-whole food processors
- polyocular linguistic-kinesthetic muddles
- equations of linear consciousness with isomorphic grapefruit
- reductionistic digital pragmatists
- intertwining relational narratives
- morphogenic negative feedback homeostats
- genetomorphic positive backfeed heterostats

Section III
- result in
- inevitably lead to
- virtually always induce
- cybernetically magnify
- actually rarely derive from
- fundamentally mediate
- can confusingly create
- often creatively obfuscate
- may synergistically adumbrate
- tend to harmonically orchestrate
- typically give rise to dissolving yet narratively interwoven
- confuse

Section IV
- diagnostically-based meaning systems
- abductive antithetical abstractions
- fundamental pragmatic determinisms
- homeostatically purposive networks
- paradoxical ecological epistemologies
- epistemic partial lobotomies
- aesthetically-based pragmatists
- pragmatically-faced anesthetists
- decontextualized holistic cybernetics
- simultaneous dialectical explosions
- holistic resonating part-whole food processors
- polyocular linguistic-kinesthetic muddles
- equations of linear consciousness with isomorphic grapefruit
- reductionistic digital pragmatists
- intertwining relational narratives
- morphogenic negative feedback homeostats
- genetomorphic positive backfeed heterostats

All I Needed to Know about Sex . . .
I Learned from Sigmund Freud

Lulu Canard

❧ If it feels good, it's probably perverted.

❧ Ink blots are really dirty pictures.

❧ You *should* feel guilty.

❧ A penis is nothing to be envious of.

❧ Sex will get you through times without love better than love will get you through times without sex.

❧ If it isn't dirty, you're doing it wrong.

❧ Too much sex makes you crazy.

❧ Not enough sex makes you even crazier.

❧ A phallic symbol is anything that's longer than it is wide and would upset your mother.

❧ Freud's first slip came from Frederick's of Hollywood.

❧ Oedipus, shmedipus! Just so long as you love your mother.

From the Portal Publications card:
All I needed to Know about Sex I Learned from Sigmund Freud © 1992

Reprinted with permission.

All I Needed to Know about Life . . .
I Learned from my Therapist

Lulu Canard

- You should feel guilty.
- Of course you have to pay for missed appointments.
- Quit complaining and get a cat.
- If sex isn't dirty, you're doing it wrong.
- You're not really ugly. You're just funny looking.
- Reality. Try it!
- Quit blaming your mother. It's your father's fault.
- Learn to dread one day at a time.
- If you're really happy, you must be in denial.
- You're still having a lousy childhood.
- Get help.
- Being happy isn't for everyone.
- If you hear voices telling you to go to Hawaii, obey.
- Just don't think about it.
- This is as good as it gets.
- If your inner child robs a bank, it's you who will go to jail.
- Before you start a 12-step program, be sure to see a podiatrist.
- Sex is no problem, no sex is a problem.
- Only hams get cured.
- Uh-huh.

From the Portal Publications card:
All I needed to Know about Life I Learned from my Therapist © 1993

Reprinted with permission.

How to Get Published

Joel Herscovitch, Ph.D.
London, Ontario

In these days of rapidly diminishing research funds, it has become more important than ever to generate publications. According to the familiar progression:

+ve Results ➔ Publications ➔ Grants ➔ Tenure ➔ Nirvana

one first needs to obtain positive results. How is this accomplished?

1. Direct Fudge

The object here is to just make up numbers which you then plug into your hypothesis. This method is simple and efficient, but risky. Invariably, some overzealous colleague (a.k.a. "keener") will suggest that he/she was unable to replicate your findings on detecting precancerous cells using the MMPI. Shortly afterward appears the dreaded request, "Could you please send the *raw data*." This requires you to make up a lot of numbers. Unless you have access to a supercomputer, it might be best to skip this method, elegant as it is, in favor of one of the following more standard practices.

2. False Positives (who's to know?)

"False positive" refers to the fact that if you do enough statistical analyses, by chance some tests will yield significance. This is the "bread and butter" method of securing a positive result. After all, "false positives" are only considered "false" if someone else knows how many analyses you performed. So, here is what to do. Do enough analyses (. . . hundreds . . . thousands . . .) to generate a number of significant results. Shred, burn or delete non-significant findings, leaving just a few for the sake of credibility. Finally write up **Intro** and **Discussion** sections, tailoring them to your significant findings. So, for example, if you happen upon a three-way interaction between day of week, ambient temperature and shoe size, your **Intro** may begin:

> *"Review of the literature suggests that small-footed scientists working in overheated laboratories on Tuesdays have thus far been unable to detect precancerous cells using the MMPI . . . "*

Always remember the researcher's motto: ***"A false positive is just a methodological improvement in the making."***

3. Bubby Research

For all you *goyim* out there, a "bubby" is a Jewish grandmother. "Bubby Research" (BR) refers to findings which your grandmother already knew.[*] The most common usage of BR involves taking a clinical group, any clinical group, dividing it equally, and giving half relaxation therapy. The other half receives another clinical intervention, say being hit over the head with a pointy stick. Although this is generally a promising method, the recent emergence of the self-defeating and masochistic personalities has yielded paradoxical results.

4. Questionnaires/Surveys

For those of you enamored with the idea of one-stop shopping, this is your method of choice. Follow these steps:
• make up a bunch of questions in the morning
• barge into an Introductory Psychology class
• do lunch while they complete the questionnaire
• collect, score, analyze and write up in the evening

No muss, no fuss. Just in case you can't get into the class that morning (say they are having a mid-term barfing contest), you need not waste time. Instead of waiting you can write it up leaving scoring, analysis and number plugging for the evening. There are two factors to consider when using this method:

> **Wording of Questions** — It is imperative to word the questions to give you the answers you want. For example, here is the translation from a recent referendum question:
> *"You're not the kind of chickenshit slimeball who wishes to remain subject to the colonialist-pig establishment, ARE YOU?"*

> **Compliant Subjects** — Just as important is having compliant subjects. This is why virtually all psychology research utilizes first-year undergraduates, whose serum alcohol hovers around moribund/comatose levels. This eliminates such "variance producing" problems as choice and free will, which intrude when using other populations, such as the white rat.

5. Reuse/Rename/Recycle

The three R's are rapidly becoming the "veni, vidi, vici" of today's modern scientist. Just because you did only one study does not mean you have to settle for one measly publication. Divide and conquer — Part I, Part II . . . voilà, multiple pubs.

[*]See *Wearing a Jacket: Protection Against the Common Cold Virus*
Mrs. Yetta Ginsberg; South Florida Journal of Bubby Research,
1985, 1986, 1987, 1988 . . .

Or you could try the "mix and match." Dig out some old data, blend with some new and with the right spin you can have an instant submission. Of course, the simplest method is the cosmetic title change.*

Oral presentations offer a myriad of opportunities. Let us say you have just presented your research entitled:

Detecting Pre-Cancerous Cells Using the MMPI

at hospital rounds. Now, when you present the same findings at a conference, **change the name**. For this, you may find use of the colon handy (not that kind, this kind ':'). Now your presentation is entitled:

Pre-Cancerous Cells: Detection with the MMPI

Then you discover that this conference is publishing a book of abstracts based on the presentations. Gravy. Now if you are are really daring, use a question along with the colon, as in:

The MMPI: Can It Detect Pre-Cancerous Cells?

Three for the price of one. Can you afford *not* to use this method?

6. Tack On Your Name (you can call me "al.")
In response to pressure to publish, gaggles of researchers are increasingly banding together in "secret societies" whose members solemnly swear to affix the names of *all* others, should *any* of them have any graduate students who do *any* research whatsoever. Unfortunately, the situation has started to get a little out of hand causing the APA to issue Ethical Principle No. 783,432 which states quite emphatically, "The number of authors of a scientific publication ought not to exceed the number of words in the aforementioned publication's abstract."

7. Your Last Resort
Finally, if you still find yourself longing for a "quick fix" for the rejection blues, you can always take the situation in hand, and like certain creative opportunists, start your own journal. For further information, contact the editor of the ***Psychlllogical Bulletin***.

* see by this author,
Ethical Principles of Psychologists: An Update
Journal of Polymorphous Perversity, 2(2), 1985, and
Ethical Principles of Psychotherapy
Psychlllogical Bulletin, Volume 2, Winter 1995

Auntie Sigmunda's Angst Column

Alistair Munro, M.D.
Halifax, Nova Scotia

❦ Dear Auntie Sigmunda:
What is psycho-oralysis?
Psychoanalysis, with less of an emphasis on the anal element.

❦ Dear Auntie Sigmunda:
Can you describe passive-aggressiveness to me?
How can such a nice person ask such a schmucky question?

❦ Dear Auntie Sigmunda:
How complex was Oedipus?
His father was dying to find out, but only his mother knew for certain.

❦ Dear Auntie Sigmunda:
What is a conversion symptom?
It occurs when you are born again, but suffer brain damage in the birth process.

❦ Dear Auntie Sigmunda:
What is sex?
That which comes between fünf and sieben in my homeland.

❦ Dear Auntie Sigmunda:
What is masturbation?
Penile servitude.

❦ Dear Auntie Sigmunda:
What is meant by concrete thinking?
I simply can't imagine.

❦ Dear Auntie Sigmunda:
Can you describe poverty of thought?
"___"

Murphy's Laws of Higher Education

Ken West, Ph.D. & Edward Polloway, Ed.D.
Lynchburg, Virginia

Murphy (1952; Cole, 1955) first identified certain truths about human existence that have since received universal acclaim (Allen & Burns, 1958; Gump, 1994). A little-known and obscure document written by Murphy contains a study of the psychological laws operative in higher education. Murphy, following his own law, lost the manuscript and later found it inadvertently circulated as a graduate philosophy exam. It was rescued by the authors who submit it here for publication.

1. The student who signs up late for class and requests special permission to enroll — with a promise of eternal gratitude — will punish the instructor throughout the year by continuing to demand special arrangements for late assignments, missed classes and unavoidable conflicts on exam nights. The promised eternity will thus be incredibly brief.

2. The student who is a quick learner and a pleaser will be praised and encouraged by instructors to the point where he or she neither sees the need to do the work assigned to the "regular students" nor the necessity of turning in assignments when due.

3. The stack of unfinished work on your desk remains at a constant height until the last student leaves campus after graduation.

4. Twenty minutes after your last paper is graded, a late paper will be submitted by mail. It will come from the student referenced above in #1 or #2.

5. The absence of appointments and faculty meetings on your calendar will always be balanced by an unexpected increase in phone calls and drop-in traffic. That is, a noxious gas always expands to fill the volume available.

6. When a student advisee confides that he or she had a boring last semester, you will suddenly recall that he or she was enrolled in two of your courses.

7. If a son or daughter of one of your friends enrolls in your course, he or she will turn out to be mediocre at best.

8. Whenever students come to you to complain about another professor, consider first whose office they just left before discussing your merits.

9. Whenever senior or graduate students bring their parents to an advisor/advisee session, enroll these students in someone else's class.

10. Students who complain about the lack of personal interaction between faculty and students will not show up at the end-of-year party at your house.

11. Whenever students swear that an uncharacteristic emergency caused them to ask for special testing arrangements or extensions (for the first time in their lives), expect additional first-time emergencies to follow in rapid succession.

12. An inverse relationship exists between the amount of help a student needs to graduate and the amount subsequently contributed to the Alumni Fund.

13. When journal editors are explicit about the changes that must be made in a manuscript, your ability to follow these instructions bears no relationship to the possible subsequent chance for publication.

14. When an editor indicates flexibility in deadlines for completion and shows little concern about specific guidelines, you will be criticized for being late and the paper will be rejected due to the lack of adherence to specific guidelines.

15. At a public presentation for your new book, the people who talk to you the longest never buy a copy.

16. The person who does the least amount of work on a committee always suggests the greatest number of changes once the task nears completion.

17. The first student in your class to address you by your first name will be the last one you would have encouraged to do so.

References

Allen, G., & Burns, G., *Reflections on Human Relationships and Cigars*
Psychology Yesterday, Vol. 93, p.123-132, 1958

Gump, F., *Mama's Understanding of Inevitable Life Events*
Alabama Journal of Looking at Half a Glass of Water, Vol. 1, p.1-2, 1994

Murphy, G.C., A *Corollary to My Law: Feces Happens*
Bitter Homes and Gardens, p.145-149, July 1952

Cole's Law, *Murphy was Not a Vegetarian*
Bulletin of Thinly Sliced Cabbage, Spring Edition, p.34-35, 1955

The Academic Landscape

Moe's Scale of Increasing Cerebral Density

1. Reservoir of Concrete Thinking
2. The Ivory Tower
3. Elaboration
4. Condescension
5. Terra Firma Academica
6. Superiority Complex
7. Paranoid Pseudocommunity
8. Bight of Passage

Section VI
Signs, Symptoms & Syndromes

Symptoms in Search of a Syndrome:
Bipolar Effective Disorder

David J. Robinson, M.D.

Introduction
Research into human motivational states recently uncovered a new illness, called the Bipolar Effective Disorder (BED). Its primary action is that of diminishing the sufferer's desire to achieve practically anything. Many afflicted with BED have been previously accused of sloth and procrastination; and in cases where marked vegetative signs are present, of being a couch potato.

Clinical Presentation
B.E.D. occurs in two variants:
• A high-energy state accompanied by scattered, superfluous activity and profuse verbal output.
• A low-energy state where an underwhelming level of exertion results in ineffectiveness. The prolonged recumbency seen in this phase can lead to an inflammatory condition called *couch potatitis*.

It is of grave concern that this condition may have both a contagious and hereditary component.

Epidemiology
Findings to date have shown BED to be a widespread disorder of significant magnitude. It seems to strike with impunity at fraudulent welfare recipients. While people of all ages are affected, a sharp increase in incidence is seen in late adolescence and in civil servants immediately preceding retirement.

Cognition
Extensive cognitive testing revealed the following "cogs" in the mindset of those with BED:

1. Don't just be an *amateur* crastinator, be a *pro* crastinator.
2. Begin a task with a day off in mind.
3. Put first things on someone else's desk.
4. Think **no/way** and find a **way/out**.
5. Seek only enough knowledge to sabotage.
6. Whenever possible, criticize.
7. As a last resort, hire a consultant to study the problem.

Etiology

This syndrome is currently thought to be a variant of the Seasonal Affective Disorder (SAD). There is a strong seasonal correlation between the low-energy phase and playoffs in professional sports, followed by high-pitched hyperbole during the off-season.

Treatment

There appears to be a therapeutic effect when subjects are exposed to the light of a television screen, though a truly beneficial effect is not seen unless they are exposed to the brightness of several screens for a prolonged period of time.

Additionally, a social skills intervention may be used in the form of repeated exposure to sitcoms. A great deal of ground can be covered in 30 minutes, which can serve as both a cognitive and family role model. Research into treatment continues, though there is strong empirical evidence that many individuals are aware of this modality and administer their own treatment.

References

V. A. Lium: **An Easier Day is Just a Few Milligrams Away**
Laid Back Press, Valley of the Dolls, California

Getcha Rest & Seeka D. Compensation:
Finding A Way to Make the Government Pay
Popular Concept Publishers; Restitution County, Ontario

Stephen R. Pogey: **The 7 Nasty Habits of Highly Ineffective People**
Federal Subsidy Press, Dole City, Nebraska

The Feral Child Syndrome

Jay R. Ryser, M.Ed., NCC-1701-D
Nagochdoches, Texas

The FERAL CHILD SYNDROME (FCS) is an often overlooked diagnosis that has been ignored and ridiculed by the psychiatric community for decades. New research indicates that this once obscure disorder may now be much more prevalent that originally thought, occurring in an estimated 89.975% of the community surveyed. The disorder requires more research to develop appropriate treatment approaches and rehabilitation. Diagnostic criteria and research methodology are included.

Introduction

FCS is the condition that humans experience after having been raised in the wild by predatory animals, usually mammals. Most documented cases involve infants raised by members of the canine species, most notably wolves, though they are not the only surrogates reported. Documented cases of infants being raised by coyotes, badgers, wolverines, bats, moles, rats, gorillas, chipmunks, hedgehogs, bobcats, raccoons, squirrels, lions, tigers, and bears* and Arkansas Razorbacks have also been publicized.

Historically, cases of FCS have met with great skepticism and have been sensationalized by both the media and animal rights groups. It was once estimated that FCS was extremely rare, occurring about once every century and then only under the most unusual of circumstances. Our research indicates that FCS is one of the most predominant psychiatric disorders seen today. Unfortunately, many cases of FCS remain undiagnosed and untreated each year because researchers and clinicians lack consistent diagnostic criteria. The author suspects that because insurance companies fail to reimburse for services to those diagnosed with FCS, the reported prevalence of this disorder is artificially low.

Research Methodology and Findings

Our own research utilized the Feral Experiences Scale with 1,867 university freshmen (male $n = 1,800$; female $n = 67$) assessing upbringing, childhood memories, hygiene and eating habits. Of the males interviewed, 93.83% indicate they were in fact Feral Children. Of the female sample, 2.9% acknowledged FCS. The reason for this disparate self-report between males and females is unknown at this time.

*Oh, my!

Anecdotal Reports

No academic work on FCS is complete without anecdotal records involving research and treatment with Feral Children. Most of the accounts of FCS in the psychiatric literature in the last two centuries deal with subjects who were only a few years old.

Cat (1992) went into great detail regarding his experimental program treating Feral Children in homogenized groups on an inpatient basis and reported many successful outcomes. Unfortunately, during the early phase of his treatment program, a radical group of Animal Rights Activists broke into the facility, freeing the subjects of this program. Most of the subjects were eventually returned to treatment, but the program was discontinued when several of the subjects attempted (unsuccessfully) to invade the sandboxes in neighborhood backyards.

Harbinger (1987), following rumors that "guerrillas" were raising a group of children in Libya, immediately flew to that area to do research, hypothesizing that children raised by primates would be more verbal than those raised by canines. His research has been published posthumously.

Laylo (1989) attempted to simulate conditions that would yield Feral Children to prove his theories regarding the etiology and maintenance of the disorder. His experiment included the use of a modified Skinner Box (full details of his research may be found in Laylo, 1992). At the time of this writing, all formal charges have been dropped by the Department of Human Services and ASPCA, and his children have now been returned to his custody pending supervision by the State.

Diagnostic Criteria

One of the reasons FCS is so poorly documented is that consistent criteria are lacking, and that clinicians are not in the habit of screening for this disorder in their usual clinical evaluations and mental status exams. Included below are the provisional diagnostic criteria for the upcoming DSM-V:

300.15 Feral Child Syndrome (FCS)

A) Having been raised by non-human parents.
B) At least four of the following behaviors are present:
1.   irritability
2.   poor table manners
3.   limited childhood memories
4.   at least one prior treatment failure

5. dirt under the fingernails
6. grunting in response to questions
7. howling at the moon
8. leg hugging
9. fire hydrant urination or urinary territory marking
10. refusal to come when called
11. excessive facial hair (e.g. mutton-chop sideburns)

Differential Diagnosis

Another reason FCS remains obscure is that many of its presenting symptoms are confused with other (and previously regarded as more common) psychiatric disorders. As an aid to establishing a differential diagnosis, key DSM-IV conditions are listed with the corresponding FCS behavior.

GENERALIZED ANXIETY DISORDER: There is a high incidence of anxiety disorders among Feral Children. The most common form of GAD is "nipple anxiety," in which a subject relives the trauma of attempting to suckle and compete among eight other litter-mates.

OBSESSIVE-COMPULSIVE DISORDER: Upon closer examination and evaluation, those diagnosed with Obsessive Compulsive Disorder are frequently Feral Children. Most notably, those raised by squirrels are found to suffer from OCD (Hoarding Type). Those raised by raccoons often demonstrate the behaviors of washing and checking.

SCHIZOPHRENIA, CATATONIC TYPE: Feral Children raised by possums can be misdiagnosed and left with the stigma of a chronic mental illness.

SEASONAL AFFECTIVE DISORDER: Emulating the habits of their ursine parents, the Feral Children of bears may be misdiagnosed with this disorder when in fact they are merely trying to hibernate.

ELECTIVE MUTISM: This can be a result of living with any number of non-human surrogate parents.

COPROPHILIA: As noted by Barfnagle (1985), Feral Children raised by canines often enjoy romps through compost and other fecal material, and frequently engage in mating rituals afterwards. See also *Leg Hugging*.

Zᴏᴏᴘʜɪʟɪᴀ: Upon further investigation, it has been discovered that many adults diagnosed as "perverts" are often only acting upon natural and irresistible impulses caused by the female estrous cycle.

Mᴜʟᴛɪᴘʟᴇ Pᴇʀsᴏɴᴀʟɪᴛʏ Dɪsᴏʀᴅᴇʀ: Not infrequently, Feral Children are diagnosed as having MPD. Inexperienced clinicians mistake the presenting symptoms for an animal alter. Also, Feral Children raised by more than one species of surrogate parent may present with different animal personalities, further complicating the clinical picture.

Aᴛᴛᴇɴᴛɪᴏɴ Dᴇғɪᴄɪᴛ Dɪsᴏʀᴅᴇʀ: Many children, and even some adults, have been erroneously diagnosed with this common childhood condition which for the Feral Child is a byproduct of their unique upbringing. The authors have discovered that the use of a flashlight in a dark office is an excellent way of gaining attention.

Treatment

Standard treatment protocols for Feral Children have relied on behavioral methods with a proven track record for related disorders. These pamphlets are available in well-stocked pet stores. It has been noted that most Feral Children respond well to positive verbal reinforcement. The first priority in the treatment of Feral Children is to provide appropriate toilet training, which is facilitated by the judicious use of a rolled up newspaper (experienced sources indicate that the *APA Monitor* is an excellent resource for this purpose). Psychoanalytic methods have been reported ineffective partly due to patients' diminished verbal skills and also due to analysts' reluctance to allow patients on the furniture.

References

Barfnagle, B. B., *Why Dogs Really Want to Lick Your Face*
K-9 Press; New York, NY, 1985

Cat, B. A., *Weird Psychiatry*
Permanent Press; New York, NY, 1992

Harbinger, I.M., *Guerrillas in my Midst*
Soldier of Misfortune Magazine; Washington, D.C., May, 1987

Laylo, C. M., *Etiology of the Feral Child Syndrome*
Hohum Press; New York, NY, 1989

Laylo, C. M., *State of California vs. Laylo*
Court transcripts and Children's Aid casefile, 1992

Feral Experiences Scale

The following instrument is designed to measure the symptoms of FCS. Please answer the questions as accurately as possible scoring **one (1) for each true statement.** Questions can be scratched into the table at the end of the test.

(1)   I like being outside.
(2)   I eat with my hands.
(3)   I scratch myself wherever and whenever I have an itch.
(4)   I clean my food before I eat it.
(5)   Large predatory animals frighten me.
(6)   I have dirt under my nails.
(7)   I answer questions with grunts.
(8)   At the dinner table, I point to what I want instead of asking.
(9)   I think of the outdoors as one big toilet.
(10) When I feel like mating, I drool, prance around and rub my private
       parts on things.
(11) I growl when someone tries to steal my fries.
(12) I enjoy lying in warm, sunny places.
(13) Fire hydrants excite me.
(14) I sleep more when the weather is cold.
(15) I eat meat.
(16) I enjoy having my back and head scratched.
(17) I howl at the full moon.
(18) I sniff my food before I eat it.
(19) I like to listen to the song, *Leader of the Pack*.
(20) If I really like someone, I smell their private parts.
(21) I wear a chain around my neck.
(22) I don't check for traffic before crossing the street.
(23) My parents were mammals.
(24) I enjoy doing things at night.
(25) I stick my head out of the window in a moving car.

Total ⬜

Scoring

21-25 You view Wolf Man Jack as kin
16-20 You run with the wolves most weekends
11-15 You occasionally wolf down your food
 6 -10 You own a *Steppenwolf* album or two
 0 - 5 You view Bambi as kin

Feral Express

Specializing in: *
• Moonlight pick-ups and drop-offs
• Rural routes
• Delivering live critters for Thanksgiving and Easter
• Bushwhacking other couriers
• Adding that "lo-tech" touch

* Not responsible for packages with edible contents.

Phenotypic Homogeneity Among Psychiatrists

Morton Rapp, M.D.
Toronto, Ontario

While attending a recent convention of the American Psychiatric Association, where about 14,000 shrinks had gathered, I suddenly realized that all psychiatrists look alike. Or, to be more exact, all psychiatrists look more like each other than like non-psychiatrists and their physical characteristics fall into identifiable categories. For example:

British Type A
• tall and lanky
• wears an ill-fitting checked jacket and striped pants
• walks as if on stilts
• scans ground as if expecting to find something of value there

British Type B
• less tall, balding
• wears a light gray jacket and baggy blue pants
• sports horn-rimmed glasses
• adopts a gaunt look

American Type
• short, stocky, graying at the temples
• if lecturing — blue business suit; if not — yachting outfit
• exudes a sense of confidence which is possible only in one in possession of a large, diversified stock portfolio

Generic Type (transcends international boundaries)
• intense-looking person of variable age, often bearded (either sex)
• variable weight, bears the worldly mien of Would-be Guru/Yogic flyer

Research Type
• no longer looks like a computer hacker with nerd-pack
• truly snappy suit with a loud but expensive designer tie — impresses bestowers of grants and lights up presentations
• still identifiable at 100 yards due to box of slides under arm

The fact that psychiatrists resemble each other so much probably accounts for the experience I have at every major psychiatric meeting — of seeing "look-alikes," that is, people who look like specific acquaintances but are actually someone else. This phenomenon can lead to some predictable but hilarious behavior. For example, I see a "John Smith" phenotype and start to approach him, smiling and extending my hand. Then, I realize he isn't John Smith at all, and what he sees is this total stranger who almost came up and shook hands with him but stopped with a frozen smile and went off somewhere else. He might start to wonder about his breath.

Alternatively I might just find myself staring at the person for a much longer period of time than one ordinarily would. This can be a rather dangerous move nowadays, especially if the look-alike is a woman. I have also been "recognized" a couple of times when others mistook me for someone else, so I was on the receiving end of the stare, double take or truncated smile.

This set me to wondering how often two people would simultaneously mistake a stranger for someone they know. The probability of there being such a pair of people at the convention is, of course, the product of the probabilities of either of them being there. But the probability of their running into each other depends on factors such as the size of the meeting, the regularity of their attendance and other issues which don't lend themselves well to simple mathematics. But let's say it can happen. Imagine the mix-up! Two people would approach each other, smiling and extending their hands. Then one or the other would recognize the error and cool down rapidly. The second would quickly do the same. Then each would find himself wondering what to say. The simplest, of course, would be, "Oh, sorry, I mistook you for someone else." But this would be too simple for a psychiatrist, so it is more likely that each one will walk off thinking the other should have stayed a patient.

I have given you but four examples of psychiatrist types; there are probably a few others. Are there features common to all psychiatrists? A few. First, all of them have eschewed the pipe, so popular in the sixties, because of the cancer scare and bolstered by the fear of being lynched by the politically correct mob.

All psychiatrists, when talking among themselves, have an earnest, pained expression possible only in someone who thinks he is tolerating an idiot who just won't listen. And finally, they all talk with their hands, like agnostic Talmudic scholars, if there is such a thing. When not talking, especially when alone and thinking they are not being observed, psychiatrists all have a look about them suggesting not that they know it all, but that they have seen it all, which may explain the phenotypic homogeneity described here.

A Clinical Syndrome in Britain:
Roundabout Induced Psychosis

Michael F. Shaughnessy, Ph.D.
Portales, New Mexico

Periodically, new clinical syndromes come to the attention of mental health professionals. A new syndrome that has been delineated (particularly among North American tourists in Britain) is that of **Roundabout Induced Psychosis**. This affects those drivers who are used to driving on the "right" side of the road (both morally and in handedness).

The syndrome begins when travelers enter their rental car. When they initially try to find the steering wheel, they soon learn that it has, as if by Merlin's magic, been moved to the other side of the car. This visual hallucination must soon become adopted as reality.

Next, the driver is faced with the dilemma a having to use the left or "wrong" hand to shift gears. The disillusionment continues as British motorists do not use their horns to signal a warning, but instead flash their lights repeatedly. The visual hallucination of flashing lights must also be quickly accepted as reality in order to continue one's vacation. The signs on British roads contribute to cognitive disequilibration and disequilibrium (distinct as they are). Unusual postings on road signs tell motorists to:

> ADJUST YOUR CAMBER
> BEWARE OF CAMEMBERT
> READJUST YOUR PRIORITIES

While British motorists check the soft shoulder and down-shift gears, North Americans are left in a state of cognitive dissonance. Cyclists, and in particular Rapid Psychlers, further contribute to the confusion and chaos of driving in Britain due to both the narrow roads and narrow focus. The illusion of elongated roads contributes to the ongoing perceptual distortion.

The final contributing factor is what is termed the "roundabout." This phenomenon is heralded by a circular sign with spikes on it. As one is supposed to yield to those on the right, motorists in the left lane may never escape the circular confusion. One is either on the left or right, as there is no middle of the road in Britain. The greater the number of revolutions made on a roundabout, the greater the chance of psychosis. While treatment has yet to be established, two common interim remedies are:
i) drive the car backwards to the nearest airport, or
ii) take the **Chunnel** to France

Psychiatric Psyntax

Cathy Mallory, R.N.
London, Ontario

❦ Q-Sign

General Medicine: The wide-open mouth of a
snoring patient (O-sign), with the addition of a
protruding tongue (Q-Sign).

Psychiatry: *Quilt-Sign*; an ominous clinical sign
indicating that a large, comfy quilt was admitted to
hospital, along with its Cluster B Personality owner,
for an extended inpatient stay.

O-Sign   **Q-Sign**

❦ TB

General Medicine: Tuberculosis.

Psychiatry: *Teddy Bear* Sign; also known as a *Transitional
Teddy*. This is frequently observed with the Q-Sign. These
cuddly and assiduous companions reduce separation anxiety
and remain a standard prop in transitional relatedness.

❦ NB

General Medicine: Nota bene — take notice.

Psychiatry: *Narcissistic Blow*; this occurs when an ego-
maniac suffers rejection, with a subsequent inability to
assimilate the meaning of life without an audience.

❦ DNA

General Medicine: Deoxyribonucleic Acid, the building
blocks of genetic material.

Psychiatry: *Do Not Admit*; this applies to recidivists and
other disordered personalities with excessive dependency
needs and who have trouble controlling their primitive
impulses.

Why did the chicken really cross the road?

David J. Robinson, M.D.

○ Autoeroticism ○ Egged On ○ Dyspepsia
○ Fowl Mood ○ Kentucky Fried Delusion ○ No Pepsia
○ Death Instinct ○ Command Hallucination ○ Fowl Territory

Autoneurotica

David J. Robinson, M.D.

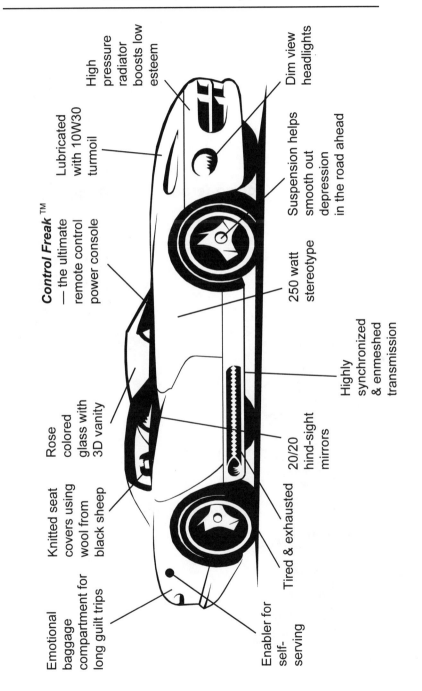

High pressure radiator boosts low esteem

Dim view headlights

Lubricated with 10W30 turmoil

Suspension helps smooth out depression in the road ahead

Control Freak ™ — the ultimate remote control power console

250 watt stereotype

Rose colored glass with 3D vanity

Highly synchronized & enmeshed transmission

Knitted seat covers using wool from black sheep

20/20 hind-sight mirrors

Emotional baggage compartment for long guilt trips

Tired & exhausted

Enabler for self-serving

Diagnostic Dilemmas

David J. Robinson, M.D.

Schizo-fern-ia ?

Vegetable Signs ?

Generation X Delusions

David J. Robinson, M.D.

- I served in the regiment commanded by Colonel Sanders in the Great Chicken War.

- The dots and dashes on the highways are a secret message in Morse Code that I alone must decipher.

- I was the leading supplier of smoked salmon to the city's delis until I inhaled too many fish-bits into my lungs.

- Somebody urinated in my genetic pool.

- My career did not start in the usual way; I was commissioned by the Star Fleet Academy.

- There is a rotund man in a red suit who sees my therapist before I do. He has a fear of crawling down small chimneys on Christmas Eve. I think he suffers from **santaclaustrophobia**.

- Every now and then a voice commands me to go to the golf driving range to hit a bucket of chicken.

- My career as an arsonist came to an end when I was apprehended for trying to start fires in a rainforest.

- My imaginary companion parlayed my childhood fantasies into a multi-billion dollar burger franchise.

- I was never happy being depressed.

- I am the world's most unfortunate Multiple Personality victim — each alter has its own personality disorder.

- I lost a bet that I could quit gambling.

- They named a medical syndrome after me. It's called the **Generation X Triad**: *alcohol ingestion, priapism and amnesia*.

Word Salad Bar Menu

The World Famous Word Salad Bar Salad Bar Salad
The house specialty! You'll feel totally verbigerated after one try.
Feel free to perseverate and return for seconds.

Thought Block Cheese Nibblers
The perfect appetizer when conversation becomes impossible.

Bouillabaisse d'Erotomanique
Prepared uniquely & discreetly just for you by a famous chef and political figure.
Feel free to track him down to give your thanks.

The Awful Falafel
For those with a persecutory bent, this one comes directly from
Saddam's Kitchen. No gustatory illusion here — it really is bad.

The Echolalia Shellfish Platter
No need to keep asking for more, tell us once and we'll
replenish your supply all night. Say, didn't you have this last time?

Capgras Vegetable Platter
Accept no substitutions! Hey, is that your *real* waiter?

Nonchalata
Our Mexican feature. It's filling, but no big deal.

The Dessert of Reference
Let your ideas take flight with our dessert specials. Still not sure?
Isn't that the voice of our manager commanding you to give one a try?

Service a
little slow?
Our maitre d'
receives
thought
broadcasts
on all channels.

David J. Robinson, M.D.

Nouveau Eating Disorders

David J. Robinson, M.D.

Abulia (Decreased willpower)

+

Bulimia Nervosa (Episodic, rapid consumption of food, often followed by purging)

=

Abulia Nervosa (A disorder where large amounts of food are ingested quickly, but with no energy to dispose of it)

Anoxia (A very low amount of oxygen in the body)

+

Anorexia Nervosa (Willful restriction of food intake)

=

Anoxia Nervosa (Willful restriction of breathing)

Ruminant (A cud-chewing, cloven-hoofed quadruped)

+

Rumination Disorder (Repeated regurgitation)

=

Ruminatiant (One who chews mental cud)

Proposed DSM-V

David J. Robinson, M.D.

Mr. Happy

Mr. Sad

Mr. Hyper

Mr. Worry Wart

Ms. Miserable

Ms. Doubtful

Mr. Vigilant

Ms. Grumpy

Mr. Complainer

Mr. Angry

Mr. Know-It-All

Mr. Shy

Ms. Flirt

Ms. Needy

Ms. Bizarre

Mr. Libido

Mr. Faker

Ms. Innocent

Mr. Scrambled

Mr. Bad

Section VII
Psychological Testing

The Wobegon Intelligence Test

Michael F. Shaughnessy, Ph.D. & Jack Moore
Portales, New Mexico

Lake Wobegon is a fictitious community created by Minnesota radio personality and writer Garrison Keillor. The people in this town are remarkable for many qualities — the women are all strong, the men are all good looking and the children are all of above average intelligence. This last point piqued the curiosity of the authors, a psychologist and a school principal.

The benefits of this good fortune are readily apparent. Shame, prejudice and despair are unknown to these children, who all seem to live happily ever after. Truancy is non-existent, teachers are relieved at not having to fail any students and special education classes (especially for the dreaded dyslexia/lysdexia syndrome) are not required. In order to spread this state of community bliss, the actual test by which the Wobegon Wunderkids achieved their superlative status is reprinted here. **The Wobegon Intelligence Test** (T.W.I.T.) essentially eliminates developmental delays, saves paperwork and frees up counsellors' time — all without the added burdens of validity or reliability. T.W.I.T is divided into four parts, which can be given sequentially depending on how far above average parents want their children to be.

Question 1
  Lake Wobegon is —
  a) A lake.
  a) The place I call home.
  a) The apex of the Bermuda Triangle.
  a) Where ex-vice-president Dan Quayle spent most of his daydreams.

Question 2
  Who is buried in Grant's Tomb?
  b) Garrison Keillor.
  b) Ali Baba.
  b) Villains from Steven King novels.
  b) Grant.

Bonus Question
  To which Grant are we referring?
  c) Foster Grant.
  c) Amy Grant.
  c) Hugh Grant.
  c) Research Grant.

Question 3

What is the name Plato associated with?
d) The dog that appeared in some Disney movies.
d) The planet furthest away from Lake Wobegon.
d) The discoverer of philo pastry.
d) The scrunchy stuff you can form with your hands.

Question 4

According to Mother Goose, Monday's child is full of —
e) Woe.
e) Granola.
e) Irony.
e) Garlic.

Answer Key
Question 1 — correct answer is (a).
Question 2 — correct answer is (b).
Bonus Question — correct answer is (c).
Question 3 — correct answer is (d).
Question 4 — correct answer is (e).

Scoring
Number of correct answers:
0 Above Average Intelligence
1 Significantly Above Average Intelligence
2 Well Above Average Intelligence
3 Really Above Average Intelligence
4 Above Average Intelligence and Beyond Superlatives
5 Above Average Intelligence and Well Beyond Superlatives

Comment
Use of T.W.I.T outside Lake Wobegon confirmed that the test shows absolutely no reliability or validity, but that it is:
• fun
• recommended by most dentists for children over the age of four
• in keeping with Lutheran values
• expected to outsell Trivial Pursuit when released as a board game
• often recycled
• composed of paper stiff enough to make excellent paper airplanes

If you agree with the premise of this article, credit the authors;
if not, blame Garrison Keillor.

Shopping by Diagnosis:
Wal-Mart as a Projective Test

David J. Robinson, M.D.

Many prior attempts have been made to develop rapid psychodiagnostic systems. Since the need to diagnose everyday behavior appears to be increasing, much effort has gone into defining the cardinal activity with which to make the determination. Though many avenues in society provide the opportunity to display one's pathology, our research found shopping to be the most fertile activity for yielding a diagnosis.

Area of Interest/Activity in Store   Diagnosis

Pharmacy

Analgesics (economy size)	Borderline Personality
Books on latest health scare	Hypochondriasis
Do-It-Yourself high colonic	Schizotypal Personality
Laxative six-pack	Bulimia Nervosa

Check Out

Exact change cashier	Obsessive-Compulsive Personality
Register nearest the exit	Antisocial Personality
Writing a check in the *Cash Only* line	Passive-Aggressive Personality

Women's Shoes and Lingerie

	If male	Paraphilia
	If female	Histrionic Personality

Housewares

Slam-Dunk mattress	Narcolepsy
Pocket food processor	Anorexia Nervosa
Industrial-size pudding maker	Dependent Personality

Parking Lot

Remains in car, orders items delivered	Schizoid Personality
Remains in car, uses periscope before exiting	Paranoid Personality
Visits only on *Customer Appreciation Day*	Avoidant Personality
Introduces self as "Wal" from Wal-Mart	Narcissistic Personality

Front Office

Thinks the PA system is a broadcast
center for command hallucinations   Schizophrenia

Sticks gum over surveillance cameras   Kleptomania

Sporting Goods

Rapid Life Cycle   Manic Episode

Wearing Goalie Mask
      With fava beans and Chianti   Cannibal
      With chainsaw   Texas Psychopath

Golf Equipment   Absolutely no pathology

My Favorite Things?

Kenneth Mah, Ph.D.
Montréal, Quebec

Sung to the tune "My Favorite Things" from "The Sound of Music"

Roaches on corpses and fungoid infections,
Mirrored self-portraits with twisted reflections.
Straight paper cuts on a bloody red tongue,
A Rorschach is bad if they see a black lung.

Transparent bodies with viscera floating,
People on fire, all blistered and bloating.
Silver-white clown-dolls with fangs and claws bare,
This kind of Rorschach would give me a scare.

When they see death, when they see pain,
That they've repressed back,
I simply interpret their inkblot response,
And then I would say, Proooooooozaaaaac!

Dwarf Inventory of Psychopathology

David J. Robinson, M.D.

The continual reclassification of diagnostic schemes means confusion for everyone. This inventory takes a more practical approach by amalgamating types of behavior into clusters, the so-called *Dwarf Prototypes*. Familiarization is available to all by way of a short story and training film.

Dwarf Prototype	Conventional Diagnosis
Sleepy	Narcolepsy, Sleep Apnea, Substance Abuse (Benzodiazepines)
Dopey	Organic Brain Syndrome, Alzheimer's Disease, Substance Abuse (Alcohol)
Bashful	Avoidant Personality Disorder, Agoraphobia, Schizoid Personality Disorder
Grumpy	Depression, Dysthymia, Borderline Personality Disorder
Sneezy	Somatoform Disorder, Conversion Disorder, Substance Abuse (Cocaine)
Doc	Narcissistic Personality Disorder, Obsessive-Compulsive Personality Disorder, Hypochondriasis
Happy	Mania, Delirium, Substance Abuse (Narcotics)

Proposed Dwarf Prototypes

Wise Ass	Antisocial Personality Disorder, Malingering, Factitious Disorder
Twinkie	Anorexia Nervosa, Bulimia Nervosa, Histrionic Personality Disorder
Frisky	Posttraumatic Stress Disorder, Attention-Deficit/Hyperactivity Disorder, Substance Abuse (Stimulants)

Geriatric Organicity Mental Evaluation Report

David J. Robinson, M.D.

The following checklist was developed using variables that have demonstrated a high empirical correlation with early cerebral organic changes when eleven (11) or more apply.

Leisure Activities
❐ Spying on the neighbors
❐ Comparing talk shows
❐ Watching the flashing "12:00" on the VCR
❐ Bingo

Favorite Beverages
❐ *Sundowner* (Tequila, Grenadine, Milk of Magnesia, Tums)
❐ *Phil's Screwdriver* (Vodka, Extra-Pulp Orange Juice, Geritol)
❐ *Holy Wallbanger* (Galliano, Cod Liver Oil, Nytol, Rolaids)
❐ *I.C.B.M.* (Ipecac, Cascara, Bran, Metamucil)

Judgment

70
This sign means:
❐ This should be the gross tonnage of your vehicle
❐ The speed limit is the square root of this number
❐ Anyone this age or older owns the road

Reading Materials
❐ Cereal packages
❐ Crime page of local newspaper
❐ **National Enquirer**
❐ **Reader's Digest** Large Type Books (the big/little picture)

Pharmacologic Fitness
❐ Shares heartworm tablet with dog
❐ Sprays roaches with antiperspirant
❐ Has five year supply of vitamins A to Z
❐ Medicine cupboard contains **Absorbine Sr.**

Self-Contained User Diagnostician

David J. Robinson, M.D.

With client-centered directives continually modifying clinical approaches, recipients of services are now sought for continued patronage as rabidly as those of a burger chain. In order to make the diagnostic process more accessible, Rapid Psychler developed the *Self-Contained User Diagnostician* (S.C.U.D.) — a comprehensive questionnaire that allows customers to select the diagnosis they want to have, and describe it using everyday terminology.

Instructions
• The questions are shown with white circles; diagnoses are in black circles.
• When you reach a black circle, look up the diagnosis on page 106.

**If you don't feel like continuing, or don't like
your diagnosis, just let the examiner know.**

① Compared to you, does the Energizer Bunny seem lazy?
No — go to ②   Don't Know — go to ②   Yes — go to ❶

② At times, do you express different sides of your personality when dealing with others?
No — go to ④   Don't Know — go to ④   Yes — go to ③

③ Could this be accounted for by the the ambivalence inherent in most relationships?
No — go to ❷   Don't Know — go to ④   Yes — go to ④

④ Do you experience intense emotional outbursts?
No — go to ⑥   Don't Know — go to ⑥   Yes — go to ⑤

⑤ Are they for any apparent reason?
No — go to ❸   Don't Know — go to ⑥   Yes — go to ❹

⑥ In which universe do you spend most of your time?
Ours — go to ⑦   Don't Know — go to ⑦   Theirs — go to ❺

⑦ Do you like to worry?
No — go to ⑨   Don't Know — go to ⑨   Yes — go to ⑧

⑧ What about?
Spiders and Snakes — go to ❻   Everything — go to ❼

⑨ Can your ultimate entertainment be purchased from a catalogue?
No — go to ⑩   Don't Know — go to ⑩   Yes — go to ❽

⑩ Are there times when your mouthwash has higher "spirits" than you do?
No — go to ①②   Don't Know — go to ①②   Yes — go to ①①

①① How often?
Once in a blue moon — go to ❾
Every moon — go to ⑩
Every full moon — go to ❶❶

①② Do you anonymously send your doctor journals on rare diseases?
No — go to ①③   Don't Know — go to ①③   Yes — go to ❶❷

①③ Do you list checking, counting or cleaning among your hobbies?
No — go to ①④   Don't Know — go to ①④   Yes — ❶❸

①④ Can you usually find someone or something to blame for your mistakes?
No — go to ❶❹   Don't Know — go to ❶❺   Yes — go to ❶❻

Diagnostic Label	**Otherwise Known as . . .**
❶ Manic Episode	Hyper
❷ Multiple Personality Disorder	Schizo
❸ Panic Disorder	Spaz Attack
❹ Intermittent Explosive Disorder	Having a Cow
❺ Dissociative Disorder	Spaced Out
❻ Simple Phobia	'Fraidy Cat
❼ Generalized Anxiety Disorder	Worry Wart
❽ Paraphilia	Pervert
❾ Depressive Disorder	Nervous Breakdown
⑩ Dysthymic Disorder	Grump
❶❶ Seasonal Affective Disorder	Jeckyll & Hyde
❶❷ Hypochondriasis	Whiner
❶❸ Obsessive-Compulsive Disorder	Nitpicker
❶❹ Self-Defeating Personality	Loser
❶❺ Denial	Taking the Fifth
❶❻ Passive-Aggressive Personality	Politician

Section VIII
Symbolism

"Object Relations?"

Descriptive Shorthand

David J. Robinson, M.D.

Complicated History	Easily Frustrated	Talkative	Day Dreamer	Competitive

Scapegoat	Politely Persistent	Believes in Reincarnation	Avoids Responsibility	Oriented

Lives Alone	Divorced	Married	Separated	Making up is Impossible

Hereditary Tendencies	Voyeuristic Tendencies	Improved in Therapy	Therapeutic Resistance	Primitive Ego Defenses

A Survivor	Gestalt Survivor	Rorschach Survivor	MMPI Survivor	Cognitive Survivor

Inhibited	Liberal	Assertiveness Training	Confabulating	Conservative

Diagnostic Shorthand

David J. Robinson, M.D.

Manic	Depressed	Rapid Cycler	Paraphilia	Narcolepsy

Diagnostic Dilemma	Chronic Fatigue	Hyperactive	Psychogenic Fugue	Somatization Disorder

Anxiety Disorder	Posttraumatic Stress	Panic Disorder	Bulimia	Anorexia

Self-Defeating Personality	Passive Aggressive	Compulsive Personality	Fractionated Personality	Multiple Personality

Dependent Personality	Histrionic Personality	Borderline Personality	Antisocial Personality	Schizoid Personality

Avoidant Personality	Schizotypal Personality	Obsessive Personality	Narcisstic Personality	Paranoid Personality

Social Work Gone Berserk:
Genogrammania I
David J. Robinson, M.D.

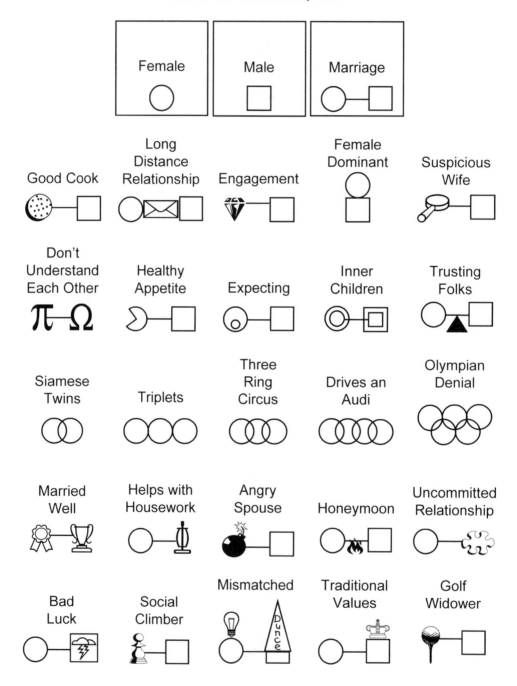

Social Work Still Berserk:
Genogrammania II
David J. Robinson, M.D.

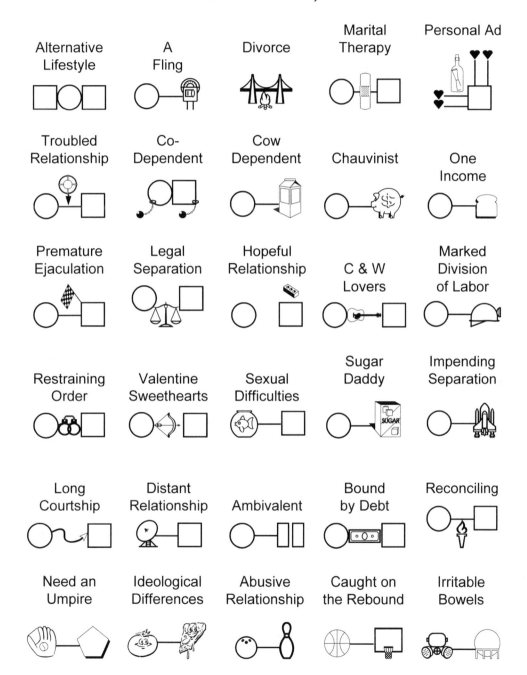

Alternative Lifestyle	A Fling	Divorce	Marital Therapy	Personal Ad
Troubled Relationship	Co-Dependent	Cow Dependent	Chauvinist	One Income
Premature Ejaculation	Legal Separation	Hopeful Relationship	C & W Lovers	Marked Division of Labor
Restraining Order	Valentine Sweethearts	Sexual Difficulties	Sugar Daddy	Impending Separation
Long Courtship	Distant Relationship	Ambivalent	Bound by Debt	Reconciling
Need an Umpire	Ideological Differences	Abusive Relationship	Caught on the Rebound	Irritable Bowels

Social Work Completely Berserk:
Genogrammania III
David J. Robinson, M.D.

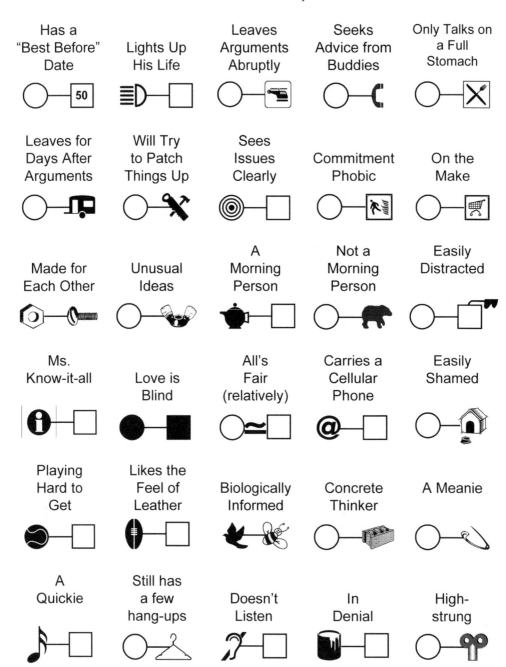

Has a "Best Before" Date	Lights Up His Life	Leaves Arguments Abruptly	Seeks Advice from Buddies	Only Talks on a Full Stomach
Leaves for Days After Arguments	Will Try to Patch Things Up	Sees Issues Clearly	Commitment Phobic	On the Make
Made for Each Other	Unusual Ideas	A Morning Person	Not a Morning Person	Easily Distracted
Ms. Know-it-all	Love is Blind	All's Fair (relatively)	Carries a Cellular Phone	Easily Shamed
Playing Hard to Get	Likes the Feel of Leather	Biologically Informed	Concrete Thinker	A Meanie
A Quickie	Still has a few hang-ups	Doesn't Listen	In Denial	High-strung

Mental "Status Symbols"

David J. Robinson, M.D.

Serial 7's Champion	Concrete Thinker	Tangential Speech	Labile Mood

Paranoid Ideas	Rigid Thinking	Completely Oriented	Financially Competent

Thought Broadcasting	Thought Insertion	Flight of Ideas	Thought Blocking

Visual Hallucination	Auditory Hallucination	Olfactory Hallucination	Gustatory Hallucination

Nihilistic Delusions	Somatic Fixation	Tactile Hallucination	Erotomanic Delusion

Wide Range of Affect	Knew Correct Age	Loud Speech	Thought Derailment

Bizarre Delusions	Well Dressed & Groomed	Knowledge Intact	Knowledge Deficient

Parking Lot of the Personality Diosordered

David J. Robinson, M.D.

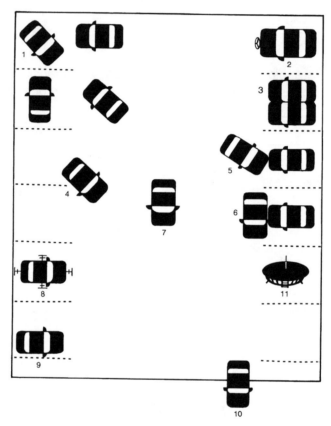

Key

1. Paranoid — Cornered again!!
2. Narcissist — Largest car; prominent hood ornament
3. Dependent — Needs other cars to feel sheltered
4. Passive-Aggressive — Angles car to take two spaces
5. Borderline — Rams into car of ex-lover
6. Antisocial — Obstructs other cars
7. Histrionic — Parks in center of lot for dramatic effect
8. Obsessive — Perfect alignment in parking spot
9. Avoidant — Hides in corner
10. Schizoid — Can't tolerate closeness to other cars
11. Schizotypal — Intergalactic parking

Section IX
Personality Disorders

The Antisocial Personality

The Antisocial Personality

Biographical Information

Name	Vinny Scumbagglia
Occupation	*Arsonist-at-large* for Fire Department
Appearance	Sideburns, muscle shirt, tattoos
Relationship with animals	Trained dog to snatch purses
Favorite Songs	*Criminal Mind, I Shot the Sheriff*
Motto	I don't mind and you don't matter

At the Therapist's Office

Before Session	Robs pharmacy in the lobby
Waiting Room Reading	Steals magazines; leaves old copies of **Playboy**, sans centerfold
During Session	Starts sentences with "@#$%^&!*"
Fantasies Involve	Seducing probation officer
Relationship with Therapist	Picks pocket, uses long distance phone card
Behavior During Session	Carves up armrest, finds *Histrionic's* phone number in the seat
Takes to Therapy	Brochure for a car alarm (that he knows how to dismantle)

Diagnostic Shorthand

Aggressive

We met in the **Uomo** Menswear store; he had to steal a tie for his probation hearing. Blunt and direct, he was a man of few words, most of them with four letters.

Slick

He said I could call him Ted, Billy Ray, or Freddy — he had i.d. for each name. The sex was fast, furious and always in a public place. He missed his other girlfriend, and got her to join us after threatening to turn in her dealer.

Predatory

He wanted to commemorate the occasion with matching tattoos - black scorpions. It complemented the ones he already had - **NFA** on his left arm and **NRA** on the right. He promised the artist payment next week, but ended up ripping him off anyway.

Dangerous

We skipped his AA meeting; it only drove him to drink, and drive. So we did, racing another stolen car into the sunset. He handled it all like a pro — and said so.

Balls

The cologne for real men

Fill-in-the-blank Personalities:
Anatomy of a James Bond Adventure

Act I
Bond, a government-contracted **antisocial**, is summoned from some exotic locale where he is risking his life recreationally instead of in the line of duty. His sadistic, **schizoid** boss, who has never even set foot outside the building to serve England, briefs him on an impossibly dangerous mission.

Bond picks up a great new gadget from the **schizotypal** in the research department. Though it is cumbersome and the instructions are tedious, it inevitably saves his life - only after he tries it out on a lowly **obsessive** sap from elsewhere in the department.

Act II
Bond quickly dumps his **dependent** girlfriend, who actually portrayed the **histrionic** in the last adventure. His itinerary is abruptly changed when his boss's **passive-aggressive** secretary uses his plane tickets for her own vacation.

Act III
After arriving first class at an even more interesting destination than originally planned, he is enamored by the charms of the **borderline** sent by his nemesis. Although she plans to kill him, Bond's superficial charm persuades her to switch allegiances. In doing so, she pays with her life but not before revealing the identity of a gorgeous **avoidant** who is the right-hand assistant to the bad guy.

Act IV
Bond enlists the help of the local **paranoid** FBI/CIA/IRA/IBM/IRS agent with a soft spot for assisting the British. Though Bond prefers to work alone, the assistance he is invariably forced to accept enables him to defeat the evil empire built by the megalomaniac **narcissist**, and return the world to safety.

David J. Robinson, M.D.

Sociopathy 101

David J. Robinson, M.D.

Introduction — Erik Erickson developed the now familiar stages of his Life Cycle Theory. In one of his first applications, he compared the anomalous development of the Singleton twins, one of whom called in a bomb threat the very night his brother was to receive the Nobel Peace Prize.

Normal (Nobel Prize)	**Antisocial** (No Prize)
Stage 1 Trust vs. Mistrust	Lust vs. Misogyny
Stage 2 Autonomy vs. Shame & Doubt	Auto Theft vs. Doubtful Shame
Stage 3 Initiative vs. Guilt	Insanity Defense vs. Guilty Plea
Stage 4 Industry vs. Inferiority	Repeat Offender vs. Reform School
Stage 5 Identity vs. Identity Confusion	Narcissism vs. Base Sincerity
Stage 6 Intimacy vs. Isolation	Gang Allegiance vs. Solitary Confinement
Stage 7 Generativity vs. Stagnation	Crime Spree vs. Collecting Pogey
Stage 8 Integrity vs. Despair	Most Wanted List vs. Two-Bit Reputation

The Avoidant Personality

The Avoidant Personality

Biographical Information

Name   Mike McMeek

Occupation   Model for "before" picture in
                                      weightlifting ads

Appearance   Matches clothes to office wallpaper

Relationship with animals   Dog introduces him to others

Favorite Song   *Born to be Mild, If You Asked Me To*

Motto   I gotta be . . . anyone but me

At the Therapist's Office

Before Session   Followed *Schizoid's* path; hoped
                                      they might meet

Waiting Room Reading   Reads nothing so as not to
                                      disappoint others

During Session   Discusses detours, off-ramps & exits

Fantasies Involve   Reincarnating Dale Carnegie as his
                                      uncle

Relationship with Therapist   Protects therapist's car from
                                      Antisocial

Behavior During Session   Spends time with head in lampshade

Takes to Therapy   *Invisible Man* comic book

Diagnostic Shorthand

The Avoidant's First Date Checklist

√ 5 packages of breath mints
√ Flowers
√ Bone for dog
√ Odor eaters (new)
√ Chocolates (good ones)
√ Cab fare home (for two)

√ Engagement ring
√ Triple-checked address
√ Food critic's review of restaurants
√ Conversation piece
√ Two watches to avoid being late
√ Picture of someone's baby

The Borderline Personality

The Borderline Personality

Biographical Information

Name	Kay Oss
Occupation	Emotional hotline counselor
Appearance	Dresses completely in black or white; today it's black
Relationship with animals	Sleeps with cat and a large assortment of teddy bears
Favorite Songs	*Love Rollercoaster, Leave Me & Die*
Motto	Come here! Go Away! Come here!

At the Therapist's Office

Before Session	Fights with ex-lover outside office
Waiting Room Reading	Castrates all pictures of men found in magazines
During Session	Smells *Histrionic's* perfume and goes into a rage
Fantasies Involve	Ménage with therapist and partner
Relationship with Therapist	Threatens blackmail over above fantasy
Behavior During Session	Widens hole made by *Antisocial*
Takes to Therapy	Suicide note, with weekly changes

Diagnostic Shorthand

Fill-in-the-blank Personalities:
Fatal Personalities Instinctively Attract

Act I

Seemingly out of nowhere, a talented, attractive and highly available **borderline** drops into the plot. A glimpse of her tortured past is given, but through a series of clever and evasive maneuvers in script-writing, the details are concealed. She quickly gets the attention of a roving **narcissist**, and lavishes on him the attention that his **dependent** wife and **schizoid** child are not supplying in sufficient quantities for his hypertrophied **ego**.

Act II

Idealization runs rampant. They live. They laugh. They love. They frolic. They "Cluster B" all over each other. They do things even a **paranoid** couldn't imagine and a **schizotypal** wouldn't predict.

Act III

Eventually things get a little rough. He needs to get back to reality, she just needs more of him. He levels with his **obsessive-compulsive** friend, who draws up a twelve-step plan for her emotional independence, but it is of no use. Erratic job performance eventually comes to the attention of his **avoidant** boss, who after empathically hearing all the details, pulls a Dilbert and fires him.

Act IV - Option 1

Admitting his stupidity to his wife causes a re-emergence of her **histrionic** side, the very qualities that drew them together in the first place. They pool their **antisocial** qualities and devise a plan to rid themselves of his **borderline** lover.

Act IV - Option 2

Events escalate to a **histrionic** pitch. He realizes life without his **borderline** lover would be dull, if she allowed him to live. Together, they make a pact not to exploit each others' **antisocial** qualities and live happily after, at least until he goes back to work.

David J. Robinson, M.D.

The Dependent Personality

The Dependent Personality

Biographical Information

Name	Anita Lott
Occupation	Food Banker & Pet Hotelier
Appearance	**Just Take Me** t-shirt under a big fuzzy sweater
Relationship with animals	Confines dog to prevent elopement
Favorite Songs	*Stand By Me, Together Forever*
Motto	Don't leave home without me

At the Therapist's Office

Before Session	Sees another therapist
Waiting Room Reading	Autographed self-help book from yet another therapist
During Session:	Describes vivid nightmares after seeing **Home Alone**
Fantasies Involve	Confining therapist to her home
Relationship with Therapist	Sits in car when *Avoidant* not there
Behavior During Session	Sits next to therapist and tape records session
Takes to Therapy	Nightly dinner invitation

Diagnostic Shorthand

The Dependent Personality
Apartment View

The Histrionic Personality

The Histrionic Personality

Biographical Information

Name	Cindi L. Valentine
Occupation	Cosmetician, Aesthetician & Beautician
Appearance	Coordinates shoes, earrings, purse, nails and accessories
Relationship with animals	Has cats named Puffy, Buffy & Muffy
Favorite Songs	*Love Me Tender, Love Potion #9*
Motto	It's not how you feel, it's how you look

At the Therapist's Office

Before Session	Flirts with others in the waiting room
Waiting Room Reading	Does quiz from a fashion magazine
During Session	Gives the quiz results to therapist
Fantasies Involve	Becoming a radio sex therapist
Relationship with Therapist	Writes best-selling novel based on sex fantasies with therapist
Behavior During Session	Faints when quiz results interpreted
Takes to Therapy	Hides a perfumed business card in the seat cushion

Diagnostic Shorthand

You've got a *hectic* day !!
A hair appointment at 10 downtown, nails at 11 uptown
and a power luncheon at 12 cross-town . . .
You've got greetings, eatings & meetings all afternoon . . .

You have to make an impression, you
simply *must!!* Whatever you do, do it ***El flagrante!!***
That's your trademark, and you have to look good
doing it!! You need makeup that won't let you down
when you're in the spotlight . . .

Dramatique

Cosmetics for the woman who wants to leave an impression,
not just a calling card.
live it . . . wear it . . . live it . . .wear it . . . live it . . . wear it . . . live it . . .wear it . . .

Fill-in-the-blank Personalities:
Anatomy of a Romance Novel

Act I

A beautiful, unspoiled **histrionic** lives a marginal and repressed existence under the cruel tyranny of her husband. However, she gave her word at the altar and remains deeply committed to this **schizoid** lout, even if he is just a shell of the man she married. His distant manner and frequent business trips don't arouse her suspicions until she is tipped off by his **paranoid** secretary that he is having an affair (with the same woman who broke up her own marriage). She seeks the comfort of her hapless **obsessive** boss who, seeing an opportunity, cannot contain himself and confesses his undying love for her.

Act II

Reeling from the betrayal of this trusted friendship, she enters a trance-like state and wastes away in her still elegantly fashioned apartment. In the nick of time, her trusty **dependent** confidante offers her a platitude which depresses her even more. Using her last ounce of strength, she sets out on a journey of recovery. Taking the advice of a **schizotypal** fortune-teller, she leaves for a distant, enchanting land.

Act III

The heat and lush, undulating landscape cause her to let down her guard and fall prey to the affections of a dashing, wealthy **narcissist**. Unbeknownst to her, libidinal strivings are simultaneously aroused in this man's nefarious, but strikingly handsome, **antisocial** brother. While being royally courted by these two, she catches a glimpse of a kindred spirit, the mysterious **avoidant** who works as a stable-hand.

Act IV

The long-seated rivalry between the two brothers reaches a fever pitch and they agree their dignity can only be settled by a duel. As high noon approaches on the appointed day, the **borderline** ex-lover of one of the brothers returns and quells his ire with her own passion. Besides, the **passive-aggressive** matriarch of the family was fed up with her ill-tempered sons and loaded blanks in their dueling pistols. As our heroine takes up with her man of mystique, clouds the shape of wedding bells form on the horizon.

The Narcissistic Personality

The Narcissistic Personality

Biographical Information

Name	James Pond
Occupation	Window dresser for a fashion store
Appearance	Silk suit, cubic zirconium cufflinks & tie pin, alligator shoes
Relationship with animals	Walks friend's Afghan in order to meet women
Favorite Song	*King of the Road*
Motto	After me, you come first

At the Therapist's Office

Before Session	Preens with a portable mirror
Waiting Room Reading	*GQ*; tells others he be featured in the the next issue
During Session	Starts each sentence with, "I . . ."
Fantasies Involve	Wonders what he's like in bed
Relationship with Therapist	Self-appointed fashion consultant
Behavior During Session	Acts as if session is being filmed
Takes to Therapy	A discount coupon for the store where he works

Diagnostic Shorthand

InnerSpace
the interpersonal frontier . . .

This is the saga of the voyager *Narcissus*,
on a five year journey to seek a way out of the . . .

Egocentric Universe

Episode 1
Narcissus has a rendezvous with *Comet Kohutek*, encountering an empathic betazoid species who mirror the prime directive.

Episode 2
Full battle stations as *Narcissus* grapples with *Darth Kernberg*, and must make use of all the ship's defensive capabilities to avoid a photon interpretation.

The Obsessive-Compulsive Personality

The Obsessive-Compulsive Personality

Biographical Information

Name	R. Lloyd Micron
Occupation	Molecule counter for a chemical company
Appearance	Underwear and socks are not only starched, but ironed
Relationship with animals	Has sent dog to obedience school every year for 8 years
Favorite Song	*You'll Do It My Way*
Motto	There are rules about making rules

At the Therapist's Office

Before Session	Washes hands before and after using restroom, then washes bar of soap
Waiting Room Reading	Rearranges magazines alphabetically
During Session	Quotes from an etiquette book
Fantasies Involve	Not flushing the toilet
Relationship with Therapist	Repairs the hole in the chair with a pocket sewing kit
Behavior During Session	Demands synchronization of watches
Takes to Therapy	A bottle of *Obsession*

Diagnostic Shorthand

Rules of Order for the Malignant
Obsessive-Compulsive Personality

√ Being a Type A personality isn't good enough; strive for an A⁺.

√ When in doubt, THINK, THINK, THINK it out.

√ After taking the inkblot test, clean up some of the mess.

√ The more you do, and the faster you do it, the longer you live.

√ If it's worth doing, it's worth over-doing, *right now*!

√ The best reward for hard work is more work.

√ Encourage others to do it by the book, **your** book.

√ Perfection is the lowest standard you should accept.

√ You can get all the rest you need when you're dead.

√ The words **compromise**, **choice** and **no** are not in your vocabulary.

√ If you can't change the rules, change the game.

√ There are others like you in every organization; find them!

√ Burn the candle at both ends, and then in the middle!

David J. Robinson, M.D.

The Paranoid Personality

The Paranoid Personality

Biographical Information

Name	U. R. Plotting
Occupation	Full-time movie projectionist
Appearance	Wears glasses with rear-view mirrors
Relationship with animals	Questions his dog's fidelity
Favorite Song	*I Spy* theme song
Motto	In vigilance I trust

At the Therapist's Office

Before Session	Checks to see if he was followed
Waiting Room Reading	Authenticates therapist's diploma
During Session	Questions partner's fidelity
Fantasies Involve	Demanding a full explanation of therapist's jokes
Relationship with Therapist	Questions therapist's fidelity
Behavior During Session	Complains about lack of warmth in the office
Takes to Therapy	Scrapbook of injustice collection

Diagnostic Shorthand

Paranopoly

TAX TIME LOSE EVERY-THING

TAKE A CHANCE **?** WATCH OUT!

MEET A LAWYER NAMED SUE!!

IS SOMEONE CHEATING?

PUBLIC UTILITIES DISCONNECTS YOUR WATER AND ELECTRICITY

GO AWAY!

GET TIED TO THE B.O.

TRACK

LOSE A TURN, NEXT TIME IT'S YOUR LIFE!

The Passive-Aggressive Personality

The Passive-Aggressive Personality

Biographical Information

Name	Maxine Sass
Occupation	Somewhere in the government
Appearance	Wears black and white together
Relationship with animals	Makes dog carry its food home
Favorite Song	***By the Time I Get There You Won't Need Me Anymore***
Motto	I'll teach you to teach me

At The Therapist's Office

Before Session	Arrives late, blames *Obsessive* for changing the therapist's watch
Waiting Room Reading	Tears out interesting articles
During Session	Repeatedly interrupts therapist
Fantasies Involve	Being *gruntled*
Relationship with Therapist	Forgets health insurance card number every week
Behavior During Session	***Miss Manners*** vs. ***Terminator***
Takes to Therapy	Weekly notice of termination

Diagnostic Shorthand

The Schizoid Personality

The Schizoid Personality

Biographical Information

Name	G. O. Solo
Occupation	Toll booth collector from 1 — 7 am
Appearance	Stove-pipe pants and a circa '70's tie
Relationship with animals	Brings "best friend" to session
Favorite Songs	*Alone Again, Naturally; Solitaire*
Motto	Through email I will prevail

At the Therapist's Office

Before Session	Gets first appointment to avoid others
Waiting Room Reading	Reads *Abstract Quarterly* in hallway
During Session	Plays *Hide & Seek,* only won't seek
Fantasies Involve	Liaison with philosophy course instructor
Relationship with Therapist	Asks to play *Dungeons and Dragons*
Behavior During Session	Teeters on edge of chair (and sanity)
Takes to Therapy	Collection of mail-order catalogues

Diagnostic Shorthand

The Antiperson Antiperspirant

You're just about to do computer battle with Zorgon for control of the thirteenth level of the CyberEmpire when the doorbell rings. After avoiding your neighbors for twelve years, why would they pick today to try and meet you?

And after all you've done to ensure your privacy — working nights, eating take-out food, and choosing a basement apartment at the end of the hallway. You can run, but you'll just have to meet them tired.

Have no fear — *Eau D'Hermit* is here!!

The antiperspirant foul enough to keep everyone away.

The Schizotypal Personality

The Schizotypal Personality

Biographical Information

Name	Aldrina Q. Cosmos
Occupation	Developer for a UFO landing pad
Appearance	Tin foil hat, unpaired socks, mood ring, dress hemmed with staples
Relationship with animals	Laments pet budgie remains dead, despite séances
Favorite Song	*Dark Side of the Moon*
Motto	There are no strangers, just friends from past lives

At the Therapist's Office

Before Session	Reads palms, tea leaves and tarot cards of others in the waiting room
Waiting Room Reading	*Astrology Weekly*
During Session	Initiates session by talking to herself
Fantasies Involve	A management position with the *Thought Broadcasting Corporation*
Relationship with Therapist	Casts a spell on therapist
Behavior During Session	Plays with Voodoo Barbie doll
Takes to Therapy	An autographed copy of new book on neologisms, *"How to Call 'Em as I see 'Em"*

Diagnostic Shorthand

The Mystery of the Amulets

Did the ancients have valuable insights into modern-day life?

Could prehistoric wisdom solve today's problems?

Still bogged down in that Florida swampland deal?

Now,
in a desert
excavation site
surprisingly close to Las
Vegas, archeo-entrepreneurs
discovered amulets that contain the
wisdom of the ages. Contained within these
hieroglyphics are fundamental truths that are as
valid now as when they were inscribed, perhaps millennia ago.

AMULET **1**
Timeless advice
for travelers[¶]

AMULET **2**
Sound financial
wisdom[±]

Order today! Quantities are limited[*]

[¶] be careful when walking between parked cars
[±] a fool and his money soon part ways
[*] to the first five thousand, then we'll make more

David J. Robinson, M.D.

The Explosive Personality

The Inadequate Personality

The Asthenic Personality

The Cyclothymic Personality

The Sadistic & Masochistic Personalities

The Multiple Personality

Personalities 'R Us Corporate Structure

Senior Management

President
Narcissist

Vice-President
Paranoid

Personnel
Borderline

Middle Management

Advertising
Histrionic

Legal Department
Antisocial

Research
Schizotypal

Customer Service
Passive-Aggressive

Workforce (with preferred hours)

Dependent
Whenever Told

Obsessive
Day and Night

Schizoid
Nights Only

Avoidant
Undesirable Shifts

The Fractionated Personality Disorder

Morton Rapp, M.D.

The Multiple Personality Disorder (MPD), a malady in which "The essential feature . . . is the existence within the person of two or more distinct personalities or personality states" [1] has gained much popularity in usage among members of the clinical community. This relatively new diagnostic entity has only been in vogue during the second half of this century. It remained rare until the 1950's, when scientific advances in the area were bolstered by two critical discoveries: (1) there's a sucker born every minute, and (2) books describing MPD were ultimately highly lucrative for the authors.

Controversy has always surrounded MPD as a diagnosis. Its supporters claim that many patients who were subjected to severe child abuse early in their lives tend to evidence MPD later on, and further, that those who would challenge the validity of this claim may themselves suffer from MPD. The author feels that this diagnosis has heuristic value and presents here a related and ancillary disorder — the **Fractionated Personality Disorder** (**FPD**).

Rationale
In mathematics, every number has a reciprocal; for example, the reciprocal of 2 is 1/2. It follows logically that if individuals exist who have more than one personality, then there must be others with only a fraction of a personality in order that the fundamental equilibrium of the universe be maintained.

Empirical Base
No studies have been performed to test the hypothesis of FPD. It was felt that the intrusion of coarse methods such as standardized interviews, or the intervention of psychiatric epidemiologists, would cheapen the area of study — and possibly ruin the author's chances of success in launching his forthcoming book(s) on this exciting new diagnostic entity.

Etiology
The specter of child abuse underlies much of the FPD, as illustrated in the following case: *M.R., a 16-year-old teenager of Yuppie background, had been enjoying a successful career as a malingerer until his 16th birthday. On that date, his father refused to buy him a Jaguar Sovereign, stating that the family's second car, a 5.0-liter Mustang, would have to do. The patient had a history of abuse at the hands of his father, namely being forced to study and refrain from using LSD. M.R., upon hearing the Jaguar was a no go, immediately stopped speaking, and became a "1/3" personality, characterized by eating only desserts, sleeping 14 hours per day and attending school one day out of three.*

Clinical Features
Despite a lack of systematic study, workers in the field of FPD have identified a number of characteristic epidemiological features:

1. It afflicts all sexes.
2. It is more common in right-handed people.
3. In South-East Asia, it is more common in Asians, whereas in Europe, it is more common in whites.
4. Its highest incidence is between ages two to ninety-four.
5. It is surprisingly common among people who are in need of a clinical diagnosis to excuse some otherwise maladaptive behavior.
6. It has a high incidence among certain occupational groups (e.g. hospital administrators). It is conspicuously absent in lawyers, which suggests that these professionals may have no personality whatsoever.

Quantitative Ecology
The diagnosis of FPD lends itself to easy quantification. For example:

$$p(FPD) = N + B^{(L/D)}$$

where:
• p(FPD) is the probability of a clinical case suffering from FPD
• N is the number of current believers in the diagnostic entity
• B is the number of financially successful books on the topic to date
• L is the lurid nature of the FPD patient's history, in standard luridity units
• D is the number of detractors of the diagnostic entity (IQ > 90)

One fruitful avenue for investigation might be determining the smallest fraction of a personality to be found in an individual (e.g. from a clinician's perspective, a one-eighth personality would be four times more interesting than a one-half personality). As yet, there is no evidence to support the existence of an Exponential Personality (where the personality would be represented mathematically by two to the nth degree), or even a square root personality.

The author has described the presence of a diagnostic entity that supplements the Multiple Personality Disorder — the Fractionated Personality Disorder. The manuscripts for six books have already been completed and copyrighted by the author. A major motion picture loosely based on one of these volumes is slated for release next summer at a theatre near you. Diane Keaton will star.

[1] American Psychiatric Association, 1987, *Diagnostic and Statistical Manual of Mental Disorders*, *Third Edition Revised*, Washington, D.C.

* From the *Journal of Polymorphous Perversity*, © 1990, Wry-Bred Press, Inc. Reprinted with permission.

Newhart Was Never Like This

The ideal group may well be composed of one of each of the personality disorders. The following script shows typical, but hypothetical, interactions between the different character types.

Narcissist: Well, I . . .

Obsessive: Nice try, but I have to call the session to order first.

Passive-Aggressive: This is a group session, not a board meeting, dufus.

Obsessive: What about circulating the minutes from last week's meeting? I have an indexed, collated and cross-referenced copy for everyone right here.

Schizotypal: You're such a yin force. Try some yang foods tonight. I'll make a list for you.

Therapist: We were all here. We're well acquainted with what went on.

Passive-Aggressive: That's quite an alliteration!

Obsessive: Well, I still have my agenda to deal with (opens daytimer). I've been reading a book called **Thinking About Feelings**.

Avoidant: Gee, that sounds really interesting. I wonder if it's available through my book club? I could use my bonus points to get us all a copy, that is, if it's OK with everybody.

Antisocial: (leaning towards Avoidant) I thought that, ahem, you know, you promised those bonus points to me in exchange for . . .

Therapist: It seems that we're forgetting the policy about contact outside the group. What's going on?

Antisocial: (glaring at Avoidant to ensure silence) My time and talent is worth money! Besides, she needed a date for the Correspondence Course Reunion.

Passive-Aggressive: Liberté, Egalité, mais pas de Fraternité, mes enfants.

Schizotypal: I'm sensing some bad karma right now. . .

Borderline: You Antisocial jerk! That's where you were! I waited up all night. I was so mad I got a headache and starting taking some pain killers, and then I overdosed on them. You made me do it!

Narcissist: He's not worth it. You should look for better men. [preens and then mutters audibly] No one ever overdosed because of me.

Therapist: I thought it was clear that group rules were meant . . .

Obsessive: To be obeyed and strictly enforced.

Antisocial: To be bent, and if need be, broken. There wouldn't be rules otherwise.

Schizoid: [freezes, then takes a renewed interest in shoelaces] Uh huh.

Schizotypal: Natural laws are too complex for human understanding.

Passive-Aggressive: [shrugs] *Whatever*.

Borderline: For others to deal with.

Narcissist: To be open to interpretation.

Histrionic: [giggles] I don't know. I can't remember. Can someone remind me? A guy, maybe?

Paranoid: To watch out for . . . or else.

Dependent: To get someone to explain them to you. I need help.

Avoidant: Wha. . wha. . whatever you say. The thought of all those new people just frightened me, and that Antisocial can be such a charmer.

Passive-Aggressive: So tell us what else happened between you two, or three, I guess it is now.

Histrionic: And don't spare any details!

Therapist: We're getting away from what Obsessive was saying.

Avoidant: I'm sorry, Obsessive. Did that make you feel . . . . . . upset?

Obsessive: No, actually, I never feel anything.

Schizotypal: Do you have a horoscope in that daytimer? What's a *non-sequitur* anyway? I never took Latin, but there's voodoo in Latin America.

Narcissist: I don't think that's important right now. What makes Obsessive and his book so special tonight? I could bring a book next week. I've had a simply *horrific* week, and no time to air my concerns.

Schizotypal: I sense a split in the karma right now.

Paranoid: Is that good or bad? Both, or neither? Can it be harmful?

Borderline: Men are all the same, always me, Me, ME. Well, what about me? Guys seem so supportive at the beginning and then they just don't care. Women are the only truly nurturing beings. I hate all men.

Dependent: You're so right! I can't remember all the times I've been let down. You keep pouring yourself out and when you're in need, there's nobody there. I need some support right now to talk about this.

Schizotypal: There is an abrupt positive force descending upon us now.

Paranoid: But how long will it last? What happens next?

Borderline: I can't believe it . . . you really and truly understand me. Now that I think of it, you've always been there for me. Now that we have each other, maybe we don't need anyone else. [gets up and sits next to Dependent]

Histrionic: (gushes) I'm glad you're feeling better. I'm sooooo happy for you. I'll bring a card next week.

Obsessive: Shouldn't you at least do a feasibility study first?

Paranoid: Or at least a blood test or something?

Narcissist: Why not consider other options . . . I think you might find somebody wonderful very nearby.

Dependent: I wish I had the courage to just reach out like that.

Schizotypal: The celestial forces strongly oppose this union. The gravitational pull exerted by a Dependent Moon can only slightly alter the course of a Borderline Comet.

Passive-Aggressive: We all know it won't work. What's your opinion, Schizoid?

Schizoid: If everyone here pairs up . . . . I can be alone again.

Therapist: Our agreement was to talk about feelings, not live them out!

Antisocial: Really honey, not so fast — just like you heard here. I was planning to surprise you. The books were going to be a gift — you know how you've always wanted to study Psychology. It's just that, um, um, what's her name here, really gets going once you give her a chance. I was on the way to the hospital when I met a few old *business partners* and got side-tracked.

Avoidant: Well, it's back to fantasizing about the personal ads for me.

Therapist: We've got just a short time left. Maybe it's time to check in with Schizoid. What would you like to share with us today?

Schizoid: Uh . . . . nothing.

Narcissist: What do I have to do to get some air time here? Bring a book? Overdose? Say nothing and play with my shoelaces?

Paranoid: You've been dominating this group and my life for too long now, Narcissist. Watch out!

Obsessive: Maybe we could make a schedule for next session. I'll bring my stopwatch.

Dependent: We could extend the time of the session — an eight-hour session would only leave sixteen in the day, and then there's my other groups. . .

Antisocial: Can we divide into little groups and change partners each week?

Borderline: Sounds like you do that anyway.

Passive-Aggressive: Small things amuse small minds . . .

Histrionic: While the smaller ones take note! I read that in *Cosmo.* You sure do learn a lot in those quizzes. Maybe we can all do one. I'll bring in some old issues next week.

Narcissist: Those quizzes are far too simple for this vapid sophisticate.

Obsessive: Sometimes I think you're just so neurotic.

Passive-Aggressive: He sure is.

Narcissist: Well if I am, so are you.

Therapist: Hold that thought, and we'll start there next week.

———

Enterprising Personalities

**Captain
Narcissist**

**Mister
Obsessive**

**Doctor
Histrionic**

Section X
Holidays, Gifts & Miscellaneous Ads

Suggestions for Holiday Gift Giving:
Kevorkian's Organs

Evan G. DeRenzo, Ph.D.
Arlington, Virginia

Mitchell Handelsman, Ph.D.
Denver, Colorado

D r. Jack Kevorkian has received considerable attention in recent years for his ideas and actions regarding physician-assisted suicide. What is less known, however, is that Dr. Kevorkian has other ideas worthy of serious consideration. One of his ideas concerns a solution to the problem of the shortage of available organs for transplantation. This article presents a potential application of Kevorkian's novel solution to the organ shortage which also will make strides in solving other problems.

In his address to the National Press Club on October 27, 1992, Dr. Kevorkian proposed that body parts be available for sale, rather than through the present system of voluntary donation. Ever-conscious of spiraling medical costs, he advanced a commercialization strategy requiring no direct public funding of the process. His plan is to have the rich buy the organs. Further, when an affluent citizen needed to buy an organ for him or herself, this individual would be required to buy two; one for himself or herself, and another to give away to a needy indigent citizen.

Of course, there are obvious ethical problems with this scheme. For example, who would decide which indigent citizen will get the organ from which rich purchaser? Who decides about the sale or purchase of organs by minors? And to whom will dissatisfied customers bring back the unused portions? In this article, we tackle these issues in a manner that has clear precedents in issues ranging from the human genome project to the application of behavior therapy to institutionalized patients: we will wait until later, when tricky situations actually arise. We believe this solution to the ethical concerns raised follows in the traditions of medical, legal, psychological and business ethics. Further, given the increased availability of organs under such a scheme, we chose to follow another All-American tradition: we will adapt a questionable concept in science to a problem in the commercial world — the task of holiday shopping. Although it can be argued that holiday shopping is only a commercial problem and of little relevance to health care professionals, we believe the problem of holiday shopping bears on a critical and ubiquitous issue that appears in clinical caseloads in everything from the treatment of ulcers to marital distress: the anxiety men feel about buying gifts for their loved ones. Each holiday season marriages are destroyed even before the wrench sets, pink socks, snow tires, vacuum cleaners, paisley ties, Mr. Coffees, and blenders are completely unwrapped.

How do we solve these three related problems? We propose the creation of a whole-year holiday catalogue of organs for purchase. A tentative listing of suggested organs for various holidays appears below. *The Kevorkian's Organs Holiday Shopper's Guide* will present suggested organs that can be purchased at discounts during various holiday times. Size will seldom be a problem (can they really transplant penises?), and what could be more personal or more thoughtful? Men can deal by phone or fax with qualified health professionals, rather than having perfume sprayed on them in over-crowded department stores. And all involved will have the satisfaction of knowing that gifts to their loved ones will be helping Tiny Tims all over the country at the same time. We hope you find the *Kevorkian's Organs Holiday Shopper's Guide* the answer to your worries about those hard-to-shop-for relatives and friends and that you have happy and healthy holidays throughout the coming year.

- All Soul's Day — Feet
- April Fool's Day — Breast and Penile Implants
- Bastille Day — Gall Bladder
- Birthday — Umbilical Cord
- Boxing Day — Jaw
- Christmas — Kidneys
- Easter — Ovaries
- Father's Day — Testicles
- Feast of St. Lucy — Eyes
- Grandparent's Day — Bladder
- Immaculate Conception — Nothing
- Inauguration Day — Penis
- Labor Day — Uterus
- Memorial Day — Hippocampus
- Mother's Day — Fallopian Tubes
- National Unity Day — Corpus Callosum
- New Year's Day — Skin
- Opening Day of the Baseball Season — Shoulders, Arms, Hands
- Opening Day of the Football Season — Knees
- Palm Sunday — Hand
- Passover — (Shank) Bone
- President's Day — Tongue
- St. Patrick's Day — Liver
- St. Valentine's Day — Heart
- Sweetus Day — Taste Buds, Teeth
- Thanksgiving — Stomach
- Trinity Sunday — Ear, Nose & Throat
- Victoria Day — Hair
- Washington's Birthday — Teeth
- Yom Kippur — Combination of Fist and Heart

This man went on vacation and lost his credit card.

This man went on vacation and lost his mind.

Vacations can be a stressful time for anyone. With the rush to the airport, the delays and the adjustments you have to make at your destination, your mental health can suffer. Why take a chance on the services available elsewhere?

Rapid Psychler now offers its ExPress™ card. If you run into difficulties, we'll send out a fully trained therapist to assist you. And with our optional gold card coverage, we'll send someone with your theoretical orientation. We guarantee attention to your mental health within 24 hours, wherever you are.*

Your mind is a terrible thing to leave in another country.
Don't leave home without the **Rapid Psychler ExPress** card.

Rapid Psychler ExPress™ *To ensure peace of mind, insure a piece of your mind.*

*Void where customer cannot be located due to fugue states.

Dial-A-Dysfunction Dating Service

You're lonely and bored, looking for that special someone to "light up your life." You've tried other dating services, personals ads, singles bars, pleading and groveling, but nothing seems to work. So why not call **Dial-A-Dysfunction**, where we have a revolutionary new approach guaranteed to find you the partner you deserve? What have you got to lose? Anything is better than the miserable existence you now call a life.

Rather than matching couples by likes or dislikes, interests and hobbies, we at **Dial-A-Dysfunction** have developed a new sure-fire way of peoplematching. Since almost everyone possesses a dysfunctional personality, we believe that long-lasting relationships can be created by matching those dysfunctions. Imagine the possibilities: Find a mate whose neurosis or addiction complements or enhances your own, thereby completely eliminating the need for that New Age Pain-In-The-Ass, personal growth and change. Don't want to have to change? At **Dial-A-Dysfunction** you won't have to change or grow an inch, or your money cheerfully refunded! Our highly trained staff psychologists will administer various psychological tests, which are then fed into our **Dysfunct-O-Meter** in order to determine the type and level of your dysfunction. We will not only match you with someone possessing a *complementary dysfunction*, but also someone with the same *level* of dysfunction as yourself.

Enjoy being abandoned?
• We have a commitment phobic partner just for you!
Uncontrollably depressed?
• We'll find someone whose biorhythms sag at the same point yours do!
Narcissistic?
• We'll find someone to cater to your every whim!
Suffering from the heartbreak of satyriasis?
• We'll match you up with the nymphomaniac of your dreams!
Helplessly dependent? Stuck at a level of infantile gratification?
• We'll find that special mommy or daddy to act out those Oedipal fantasies
Yes, you too can get the partner you deserve, without having to grow an inch!

Other products available:
• "Humorously Challenged No More: *Getting The Laughs You Need*" (40 minute video)
• "12 Steps For The Humorously Challenged" (poster)
• "I'm OK But **You** Need Professional Help!" (buttons and bumper stickers)

For more information contact:
David Granirer, Tune-In Counseling Services
3633 Triumph Street, Vancouver, B.C. Canada V5K 1V4
(604) 205-9242   fax (604) 205-9243

Meeting the Diverse Needs of Clients

Jane P. Sheldon, Ph.D.
Ann Arbor, Michigan

As part of a comprehensive and holistic approach to therapy, many treatment facilities are offering programs to meet the diverse needs of clients. The following is a brief list of some of the new products and services now being offered:

❦ Day care services for inner-children

❦ 12 step aerobic classes

❦ Virtual travel agents for agoraphobics

❦ Doubles tennis tournaments for co-dependents

❦ Multiple personality monogramming services

❦ Dysfunctional family discounts at hotels and restaurants

❦ Computers with 16 megabytes of repressed memory

❦ Rapid Re-Psychling bins for unsold copies of the *Psycholllogical Bulletin*

Gift Items

Jane P. Sheldon, Ph.D.
Ann Arbor, Michigan

Co-Dependency Mug

Item 24T-T42, $12.95 each
(includes a $2 co-payment fee)

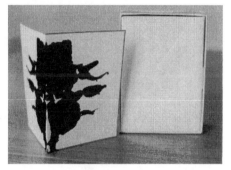

| To order any of these items call **1-800-555-DSM4** |

All-Occasion Greeting Cards

By Freudian Slip Inc.

"When you care enough to
send the very brest."

Price negotiable — what do
you think they're worth?

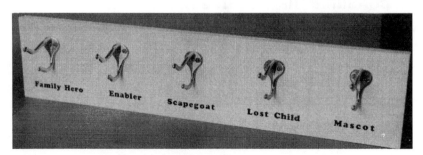

Family Hero   Enabler   Scapegoat   Lost Child   Mascot

Dysfunctional Family Coat Rack

Item #7-11 $19.99 plus $13/peg

Rabid Psychler

Cannibal Quarterly

This month:

An interview with Dr. Hannibal Lecter

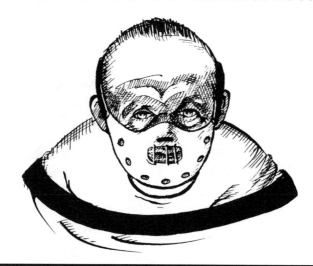

**"It made incredible sense to me . . .
if we do become what we eat, then why not
consume the wealthiest, most
beautiful and sophisticated people that
we possibly can."**

Other Articles:

☠ Liver by the River: A Mississippi Delicacy
☠ Starve a mosquito — keep your blood & be Vlad you did!
☠ Who said fish was brain food? Try the real thing!

David J. Robinson, M.D.

Melanie
~~Calvin~~ Klein

Good breasts or bad — they still need support!
Don't listen to what mother says, your first brassiere
can be crucial in your later development.

Take a position, choose *Melanie.*

David J. Robinson, M.D.

Lady Macbeth Knows Dirt

Having to worry about cleaning everything from delusional blood stains to Arabian perfume, Lady M. certainly had her hands full. We obtained her famous Dunsinane Castle formula and are now pleased to bring you our new household cleaner, ***Out, Damned Spot!***, named in honor of her ladyship.

Available, as you like it, in spray, aerosol or liquid forms.

David J. Robinson, M.D.

Editorial Bored
Psycholllogical Bulletin

September 1, 1996

Dear Bored:

I saw the announcement on Dan Rather the other evening that you are searching for a new editor for the *Psycholllogical Bulletin*. I not only wish to apply, but expect to be appointed shortly (actually, longly, for I expect to be the editor in perpetuity). I realize the current editor is being, shall we say, "erased" from his position. Because of such sound judgment, I have decided to apply to work for you instead of the **New York Times**, **Lancet**, **Time** and the **New England Journal of Medicine**, all of whom would give their linotypes to get me (I'll confess I have worked for lesser names, but that is all in the past).

I have enclosed my c.v. for your perusal. I have an excellent track record (even though I am not a race horse) with a proven ability to find and correct erors. Having left a trail of destruction behind me, I am unable to provide any references. I am extremely attuned to the faults of others and do not hesitate to point them out, which makes me a prime candidate for the position of editor. I consider it far more important to be grammatically correct than politically correct and I espouse my own view on this. Finally, I am the proud owner of an autographed copy of the **Chicago Manual Of Style**.

I shall expect to be provided safe passage via Air Canada (does it fly out of Nebraska?), and to be picked up by limousine (though in truth, I have been picked up by less in my time) and whisked to the nearest Hilton (surely you have one). I am prepared to begin my duties immediately thereafter so please secure a bored room for me to meet with the publication staff. I'd prefer the deposed editor not be present. I expect he will be vindictive, and although the pen is mightier than the sword, I don't want a pen stuck in my back either. I'd prefer to not have to use my rapier (and enough said about that!) wit to level him in front of his (by then former) colleagues.

Grammatically yours,

Norvel Nostrum, Pr.D.

by Larry Lister, D.S.W.
Kailua, Hawaii

Xmas on 2 North

Donna S. Rubin
New York

Twas the night before Xmas; it had been a long day,
Two North was quiet, yes, even C.A. !*
Most patients were warmly tucked in their beds,
It was after ten, so they'd all had their meds.

> *C.A. is the isolation area or quiet room.

At the desk sat Debbie, busy on the phone,
There were folks in the sunroom where a movie was shown.
In the dining room artwork adorned all the walls,
And earlier that day, they'd sung "Deck the Halls"

Socks were hung in the laundry room with care,
In hopes that a new dryer soon would be there.
In the kitchen lay remains of cookies and cake,
It's amazing how much of a mess people make!

A patient was crying, in need of TLC,
Another one sat, fast asleep by the TV.
The census was high; folks of all ages,
All recovering in different stages.

Suddenly, footsteps were heard to sound,
The nurses got up and began looking around.
No patient was missing, C.A. was secure,
What's going on? They couldn't be sure.

They thought, could it be, just like in the poem?
Where St. Nick visits somebody's home?
One nurse exclaimed, "We could sure use a hero!"
And who should appear but Dr. Shapiro!

Not Santa at all, just a very nice man,
Who does for his patients whatever he can.
As do all of the staff, from doctors to aides,
And they get all too few of their deserved accolades.

I give this to them, my holiday verse,
I'm a former patient, who once felt a lot worse.
To all who're admitted, try to have hope and good cheer,
Whatever solace you need, you will find it here.

However you celebrate, whatever your rite,
Happy holidays to all, and to all a good night.

The Rapid Psychler Workout

Warm-Up
♣ Open wide, place foot in mouth, then change feet

♣ Jump to conclusions

♣ Do the political side-step

Part I
♠ Cut corners

♠ Turn a blind eye

♠ Search for a scapegoat

♠ Wrestle with guilt

Nutrition Break
♦ Eat your own words

♦ Chew the fat

Part II
♥ Shrug things off

♥ Duck responsibility

♥ Pass the buck

♥ Split hairs

Nature Break
♣ Miss the forest for the trees, then the trees for the forest

♣ Be out, standing in your field

Cool Off
♠ Do the Dance of Intimacy

read the book . . . see the movie . . . play the computer game . . . hit the website . . . buy the merchandise . . . send us an email . . . check out the calendar . . . get the book on the making of the movie . . . buy the video of outtakes from the movie . . . see the movie of the writing of the book . . . purchase the hint book for the computer game . . . dial up our 900 number . . . see the live concert . . . listen to our motivational tapes . . . use our playing cards . . . get one of everything for your friends and family . . .

Collect the whole set!
Cereal Killer Cards

Voodoo Vic the Vengeful Vulture
Vic puts a voodoo curse on those
who dig out the enclosed giveaway
before the cereal box is empty.

The Quacker State Oil & Oats Man
This ruthless tycoon amalgamated
Quacker State Oil and Quacker Oats
to produce a high-octane crisp that
explodes on contact with milk.

Antonio the Sicilian Tiger
Known for his bellowing voice and loud
snarl, Antonio is sought for *frosting
over* those who interfere with the
family's breakfast business.

Captain BoneCrusher
This sadistic seadog
produces a breakfast
nugget that absorbs calcium.
He is sought for the
quasimotoric deforming of the
Crunchback of Notre Dame.

David J. Robinson, M.D.

Visit our famous Blank Screen Room!
Analytic Apparel & Accouterments

Coordinate your wardrobe, whisk, wit, wallpaper,
watch, wallabees, woolens, wallet, workbook,
water glass, writing paper, whirlpool, waffling,
wainscoting, washtub, wedding, whim
and wastebasket at our store!!

Choose your attire and matching accessories
from any of a number of shades of gray.

David J. Robinson, M.D.

Other Rapid Psychler Products

Our Holiday Card (red)

Another case of
santaclaustrophobia!

Our "What's Your Perception" Card (yellow)

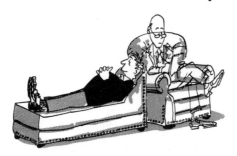

I had been seeing a therapist for
three years . . .

. . . until I realized I was just
hallucinating !

Rapid Psychler Press produces educational and humorous
publications for use in all areas of Mental Health. Our specialty is
producing texts that are comprehensively researched, well organized,
reasonably priced, clinically oriented, and include humor as an aid to
education. We also have presentation kits (slides and overheads),
seasonal and greeting cards, and a rotating line of merchandise (e.g.
shirts, shorts, memo-pads, coffee mugs, mouse-pads etc.).
Let us know if you're interested in a gift item!

DISORDERED PERSONALITIES

A PRIMER

DAVID J. ROBINSON, M.D.

Description: This is a unique new book on the basics of personality disorders that is presented in a humorous style. This primer is funny and well written and is a useful teaching tool.

Purpose: The purpose is to provide a comprehensive primer on personality disorders that is both readable and fun to read. The author has accomplished this mission.

Audience: The intended audience is medical students and psychiatry residents. Clinicians and trainees in psychology, social services, family practice, and internal medicine would also enjoy and benefit from this primer. Any clinician who cares for patients will find this an extremely useful book.

Features: The book features 288 pages containing sections on each personality disorder. Each section has a reference portion that is really a "suggested reading," since these citations are all secondary and tertiary sources. The book is filled with amusing illustrations, caricatures, and even media examples of the various personality traits, which is a good way for trainees to remember these disorders.

Assessment: This is an excellent, humorous, and useful teaching tool intended for trainees. This is definitely a fun way to learn this material.

Doody's Review

"**Disordered Personalities** is both informative and fun to read. It demonstrates that humor is useful in diagnosis, discussions with patients, and one's own awareness and self-care."

Alan D. Schmetzer, M.D.
Director of Education & Assistant Chairman
Department of Psychiatry
Indiana University School of Medicine

Disordered Personalities: A Primer

provides a comprehensive and entertaining introduction to the DSM-IV personality disorders. The information is presented in an organized and readable format, with humor integrated to make an effective and entertaining presentation. This book takes a unique approach by illustrating "textbook" concepts with examples that all readers will enjoy.

Features include:
- Explanations of diagnostic and theoretical principles
- Thorough coverage of each personality disorder
- Summaries of past personality disorders
- DSM-IV diagnostic criteria
- Caricatures by Brian Chapman
- Satirical articles from the *Psychlllogical Bulletin*

288 pages, hard-cover, ISBN 0-9680324-0-0

Disordered Personalities Presentation Set

Color presentation graphics are available
as 35mm slides and overheads.¶

***Part I — Personality Disorders — Color versions of the
illustrations at the beginning of each chapter (with headings):**

1. Schizoid   **2.** Schizotypal
3. Paranoid   **4.** Antisocial
5. Borderline   **6.** Narcissistic
7. Histrionic   **8.** Dependent
9. Obsessive-Compulsive   **10.** Avoidant
11. Passive-Aggressive   **12.** Asthenic
13. Cyclothymic   **14.** Explosive
15. Self-Defeating & Sadistic Personalities
16. Multiple Personality Disorder
17. Inadequate

*Part II — Illustrations of Theoretical and Diagnostic Principles:
18. Personality or Personality Disorder?
19. Object Relations Therapy
20. Transference/Countertransference (together in one slide)
21. Theoretical Principles (Freud Family)
22. Resistance
23. Behavior Therapy
24. Countertransference
25. Cognitive Therapy
26. Parking Lot of the Personality Disordered
27. Conflict in Ego Psychology
28. Ego Defenses
29. Organic Personality Disorder
30. Medical vs. Psychiatric Perspectives

***This package is available only as
a complete set containing Parts I & II.**

¶ Please specify slides or overheads when ordering.

Brain Calipers
A Guide to a Successful
Mental Status Exam

David J. Robinson, M.D.

*I highly recommend **Brain Calipers** to psychiatry residents, medical students, and psychiatrists preparing for their board examinations. This book is a very comprehensive review of the mental status examination. In addition to being informative, it is very readable and highly entertaining.*

Steven E. Hyler, M.D.
Associate Professor of Clinical Psychiatry
Columbia University

The Mental Status Examination (MSE) is an essential component of all clinical interviews, and remains the cornerstone of descriptive psychopathology. It is a structured set of questions and observations designed to assess:
- **Perception**
- **Thinking**
- **Feeling**
- **Behavior**
- **Cognitive Functioning & Sensorium**

Brain Calipers: A Guide to a Successful Mental Status Exam

provides a comprehensive and enjoyable overview of the psychiatric mental status exam.

Features include:
- **DSM-IV** diagnostic criteria that pertain to findings on the MSE
- Coverage of each aspect of the MSE in an individual chapter with definitions, numerous examples, and explanations outlining the relevance of specific findings
- Sample questions to ask in each section of the MSE
- An "edutainment" approach with over forty illustrations by Brian Chapman, twenty-five pages of humorous articles, numerous mnemonics and helpful summary diagrams

392 pages, soft-cover, ISBN 0-9680324-3-5

Brain Calipers
Presentation Set

Color presentation graphics are available
as 35mm slides and overheads.¶

*Part I — Color versions of the illustrations at the beginning of each chapter (with headings):

1. Mental Status Exam	**2.** Appearance
3. Behavior	**4.** Cooperation
5. Speech	**6.** Thought Process
7. Thought Content	**8.** Suicide & Homicide
9. Affect & Mood	**10.** Perception
11. Insight & Judgment	**12.** Cognitive Functioning

*Part II — Major Clinical Diagnoses (Axis I Conditions):

13. Schizophrenia	**14.** Depression
15. Mania	**16.** Anxiety Disorders
17. Sleep Disorders	**18.** Eating Disorders
19. Adjustment Disorders	**20.** Sexual Disorders
21. Dissociative Disorders	**22.** Factitious Disorders
23. Cognitive Disorders	**24.** "Organic" Conditions
25. Impulse-Control Disorders	
26. Substance Abuse Disorders	
27. Substance Dependence Disorders	
28. Substance-Induced Disorders	
29. Somatoform Disorders	
30. Medical vs. Psychiatric Perspectives	

*** This package is available only as a
complete set containing Parts I & II.**

¶ Please specify slides or overheads when ordering.

PSYCHIATRIC MNEMONICS

& CLINICAL GUIDES

David J. Robinson, M.D.

For those who are teaching Abnormal Psychology (or even Normal Psychology), this book is a great way to help students and interns deal with the Major Clinical and Personality Disorders that exist in the DSM-IV. Using funny and appropriate mnemonics, Dr. Robinson helps us to remember the essential elements of various ailments. For example, the mnemonic "**I FEAR LARD**" contains the elements of Anorexia Nervosa:
I—Image of body distorted; F—Fear of weight gain; E—Expected weight gains not made; A—Amenorrhea; R—Refusal to gain weight; L—Laxative Use (Binge-Purge Type); A—Anhedonia; R—Restricting Type; D—Denial of weight loss

For practitioners working with patients taking various medications, Dr. Robinson also provides in acrostic format, mnemonics for summarizing the side-effects of various drugs.

Throughout this book are caricatures that help students learn the various personality disorders. Also included are flow charts as well as various important "tidbits," all done in an amusing and informative style. Humor is a great way to help students learn the ABC's of the Mental Status Exam (Appearance, Behavior, Cooperation), the E.R. interview, and important organic considerations.

Not since Lazarus came up with the BASIC ID to help us remember his multimodal approach has there been such a book to help mental health professionals deal with the vast amount of material in a comprehensive way. Robinson uses humor to help us learn, remember, and ultimately to help our clients and patients better, and to make the H.M.O. process less onerous. I recommend this to P.H.D.s, M.S.W.s and M.D.s and suggest P.D.Q. they purchase this book A.S.A.P.

Michael F. Shaughnessy, Ph.D.
Professor of Psychology
Eastern New Mexico University

Psychiatric Mnemonics provides a practical and comprehensive introduction to clinical psychiatry. Mnemonics, summaries & guides are included for:
• Clinical Disorders
• Personality Disorders
• Conducting Interviews
• Mental Status Examination
• Cognitive Functioning
• Differential Diagnosis
• Medical Disorders
• Medication Side-Effects

96 pages, soft-cover, ISBN 0-9680324-1-9

The Psycholllogical Bulletin

Got an idea kicking around?

The *Psycholllogical Bulletin* welcomes submissions in both text and graphical forms. Successful authors receive a Rapid Psychler keychain and five volumes of the Bulletin in which the article is printed. Additionally, when an anthology (such as *Kick-in-the-Pants* **Therapy**) is printed, each author receives a free copy.

Articles can be submitted by mail, email or fax. Original copies of artwork must be enclosed.

Subscriptions are $10 per year, which includes two volumes (summer and winter). All subscriptions begin with the summer edition.

Journal of Polymorphous Perversity

The Journal of Polymorphous Perversity (*JPP*) publishes humorous and satirical works in the fields of Psychology, Psychiatry, and related disciplines.

Subscriptions are by volume (year) and begin with the Spring/Summer issue (i.e. all subscription orders received in 1997 automatically begin with the Spring/Summer 1997 issue)

The *JPP* welcomes submissions of articles for consideration. Contributions should be submitted in triplicate, accompanied by a self-addressed, stamped envelope. Please keep a copy of all materials submitted, we cannot take responsibility for lost materials.

Rates	1 Year	2 Years
Individuals		
United States	U.S. $ 14.00	U.S. $ 24.00
Canada & Mexico	U.S. $ 15.75	U.S. $ 28.50
Other Foreign	U.S. $ 21.75	U.S. $ 38.00
Library & Institution Rate		
United States	U.S. $ 20.00	U.S. $ 40.00
Foreign	U.S. $ 26.00	U.S. $ 52.00

The JPP is published by Wry-Bred Press, Inc.

Editorial Office
10 Waterside Plaza
Suite 20-B
New York City, NY
USA 10010
Phone: 212-689-5473
Fax: 212-689-6859

For Submissions, please send to:
Editor, JPP
Wry-Bred Press, Inc.
P.O. Box 1454
Madison Square Station
New York City, NY
USA 10159-1454

Back issues are available from Vol 1(1), Spring, 1984 onward.
Optima, Visa, Mastercard & American Express are welcome.

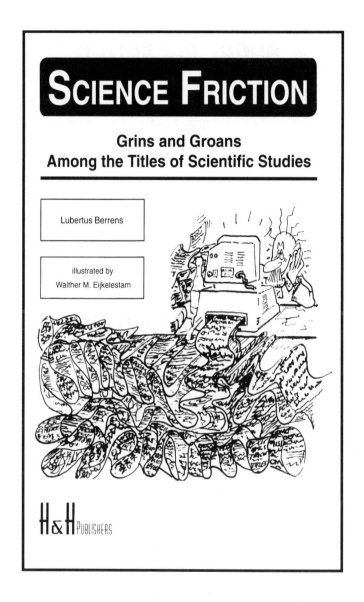

Science Friction is a collection of (real !) articles from the biomedical literature. This book contains witty commentary and drawings satirizing many of the titles. This book was written by Prof. Lubertus Berrens, illustrated by Walther Eijkelestam, and published by Hogrefe & Huber.

91 pages, soft-cover, ISBN 0-88937-146-6

About the Editor

Dave Robinson is a psychiatrist practising in London, Ontario, Canada. His particular interests are consultation-liaison psychiatry and education. A graduate of the University of Toronto Medical School, he completed a Residency in Family Practice before entering the Psychiatry Residency Program. He's a diplomat of the American Board of Psychiatry and Neurology.

His hobbies are playing the sax, computer simulation games, red-lining a Toyota MR2-Turbo, collecting Coca-Cola paraphernalia and, yes, cycling.

A former class clown, he is a potent example in the case against public education. His friends and family unanimously voted that his satirical articles should be put in print, rather than repeated whenever he has an audience.

About the Artist

Brian Chapman is a resident of Oakville, Ontario, Canada. He was born in Sussex, England and moved to Canada in 1957. His first commercial work took place during W.W. II when he traded drawings for cigarettes while serving in the British Navy. Now retired, Brian was formerly a Creative Director at Mediacom. He continues to freelance and is versatile in a wide range of media. He is a master of the caricature, and his talents are constantly in demand. He doesn't smoke anymore.

Brian is an avid swimmer and trumpeter. He performs regularly (on the trumpet, that is) in the Toronto area as a member of three bands. Brian is married to Fanny, a cook, bridge player and crossword puzzle solver extraordinaire. Brian and Fanny are Dave's godparents.

About Rapid Psychler Press

Rapid Psychler Press was founded in 1994 with the aim of producing publications that further the use of humor in mental health education. We are interested in coordinating material from other contributors that fits this format. Rapid Psychler will be specializing in producing CD-ROMs and slide and overhead sets to aid instructors, as well as continuing to publish textbooks. We exhibit at the annual meetings of major mental health organizations.